Living Life @
Its Best

Living Life @ Its Best

Where Faith and Emotional Intelligence Intersect

Allan G. Hedberg, Ph.D.

Clinical and Consulting Psychologist

authorHOUSE®

AuthorHouse™ LLC
1663 Liberty Drive
Bloomington, IN 47403
www.authorhouse.com
Phone: 1-800-839-8640

Published by AuthorHouse   10/23/2013

ISBN: 978-1-4918-1884-8 (sc)
ISBN: 978-1-4918-1885-5 (e)

Scripture taken from the Holy Bible, New International Version, Copyright 1973, 1978, 1984 Biblica. Used by permission of Zondervan. All rights reserved

Any people depicted in stock imagery provided by Thinkstock are models, and such images are being used for illustrative purposes only.
Certain stock imagery © *Thinkstock.*

This book is printed on acid-free paper.

CONTENTS

PART IV

PART V

APPENDICES

ARROW-HEADS: A Tribute to the late Rev. Fred Beck

The year was 1945. Our family of five relocated to the south side of Chicago, Illinois from Saginaw, Michigan. My father was treasurer of a flourishing tool and die company. Due to changes in ownership after a few years, he left that position to start a career in life insurance sales. I was seven years old at the time.

Our new home was in the area of 79th and State streets. Three blocks away was the Elim Evangelical Free Church, which became our church home. The pastor was the Reverend Fred Beck. To me, he was Pastor Beck.

I remember Pastor Beck very well. Each Sunday, he walked up to the platform dressed in a tuxedo, a black coat, long tails and deep gray pin striped pants. His 6" 5" frame created an impressive and confident appearance. Pastor Beck had a deep baritone voice. His voice was firm. He spoke with authority, yet, he was kind and gentle. His smile was compelling.

On my way to and from school each day, I passed the church. Elim was a stately church. A bulletin board was conspicuously placed in front of the church on which Pastor Beck announced the title of his sermon for the next Sunday. This was faithfully done on Thursday. Between Monday and Thursdays, it was his custom to also place a catchy quotation on the bulletin board. He called his thought provocative quotes, Arrowheads. He also published and discussed these quotes in a monthly article he wrote for his church's denominational newspaper, *The Evangelical Beacon.*

In 1943, Pastor Beck, in concert with Beacon Press, published a book compiling his Arrow-Heads. It was entitled, *ARROW-HEADS: Some Straight Lines for Strong Living.* These were his original quotes, 660 in total. He wrote on all kinds of subjects. The Table of Contents of the book included topics such as greed, life, happiness, selfishness, affliction, pride, vision and worry, to name a few. These were the quotes he used on the bulletin board out front of the church.

My purpose of using his quotes in this book is to recognize and preserve this collection of Pastor Beck's arrowheads and make them available once again for our instruction, enjoyment, and use. The arrowheads are brief quips, but come with a powerful message behind the quip. They are mini-lessons in daily living.

Being interpersonally smart depends on one's emotional intelligence. Emotional intelligence is comprised of 15 vital traits of social interactions and relationships. I selected from the 660 arrowheads those that illustrate each of the 15 traits of emotional intelligence. Feel free to use the arrowheads as they are helpful to you.

I express my appreciation to Mrs. Anna Rose, the daughter of Fred Beck, for allowing me the privilege of using the arrowhead quotes from her father's book as I saw fit.

Enjoy the rest of the book . . .

AGH

PREFACE

Emotional Intelligence and Personal Faith

Over the past 25 years of psychological research, emotional intelligence has been shown to play a crucial role in our relationships, productivity, performance, job satisfaction, and a lifestyle based on faith. Essentially, emotional intelligence is the basis of positive productivity, educational achievement, interpersonally engagement and focused faith. Emotional intelligence is associated with confidence, diligence, and self-respect. It is the foundation to calmness, flexibility, hope, and sustained attention when work place and family life crises hit and panic threatens to set in.

Faith is the belief in a person much greater than oneself that is influencing the events of history and the life experiences of each individual. Personal faith is the decisive act of placing one's confidence and very life in the hands of a personal God who cares and lives within those who have placed their trust in him. He is the essence of what one would hope for and the essence of things unseen. Faith is living beyond the here and now and with a view of life's purpose and meaning into the future . . . eternity.

Emotional intelligence and faith intersect when a person acts in faith and trusts the living God for wisdom when confronting a real life event, problem, or situation. Such events are faced with an expectation of positive resolve because God is in it and cares about the outcome and those involved in it. It is ultimately taking on a significant event that would fail if God were not in it. And the competencies of emotional intelligence can be well utilized in these events to obtain positive resolution.

Quite simply, emotional intelligence is a set of competencies that enhance a person's ability to relate positively to others in a wide variety of settings. It is being interpersonally smart and effective. People with high emotionally intelligence scores are adept at using empathy and constructive communication to create a collaborative and cooperative environment at home, work, church and school. As they perform in these different settings, they tend to be able to label their emotions, have a sense of appreciation for the cause and the effect of their feelings, allow the full range of emotions to be wisely expressed, and be able to moderate their feelings, privately and publicly. They are also able to understand and appreciate the role of faith and the interventions of God in all of life's daily experiences.

Emotional Intelligence and the Work Place

Tonya Harding, the famous skater, Bobby Knight, the famous coach, and Mike Tyson, the famous fighter, all had excellent trade and athletic skills, but poorly developed emotional intelligence. There are many other examples, too. Because of this, each experienced significant negative effects on their career. None finished well. It has been estimated that 27% of all workers in the work place display poor emotional intelligence, according to a report from the Center for Creative Leadership.

Because of this, employee training programs in emotional intelligence have been undertaken by many companies and organizations. Employers have found that no matter how professionally and technically skilled a worker might be, the lack of emotional intelligence simply increases cost and overhead, and robs the company of positive productivity. Poor production has also been found to spread to other employees and can create an "internal growing cancer" within a company.

Studies have shown that emotional intelligence is responsible for 58% of work performance. Those with the highest emotional intelligence make $29,000.00 more in annual salary, on the average. Approximately, 90% of the top performers in the work place have high scores on tests of emotional intelligence. It pays for employers to hire those with positive emotional intelligence and train those that lack this vital component of successful living and working.

Emotional Intelligence and the School System

Emotional intelligence can also be understood by evaluating our school system and how it deals with our children. Unfortunately, most community schools do not foster good emotional intelligence so that strong connections with friends and adults can be acquired. Research data indicates that approximately 30% of sixth through twelfth grade students report that their schools provide a caring and encouraging environment. Further, approximately 30% of high school students admit that they engage in high risk behaviors such as substance abuse, violence, acts of sexual freedom, and even suicide attempts. Overall, schools do not provide a strong and positive learning environment in which personal growth and the skills of emotional intelligence are taught, modeled, and encouraged.

On the other hand, research studies show that if schools teach students from the early grades to work well with others, regulate their emotions and constructively solve problems, the students will be better equipped to deal with life challenges, including academic challenges. Simply stated, emotional intelligence correlates strongly with interpersonal learning and academic learning. It is the responsibility of teachers, school administrators and parents to work together in harmony to oversee their children's social, emotional, and character development. Schools that create a positive school climate boost children's social competencies and learning will progress at a positive rate. In such positive environments, students also learn social competencies that contribute to their long-term social, vocational, academic and marital success.

This approach to social and emotional learning has been taught to tens of thousands of children and adolescents since the late 1980s. The teaching has been done through formal classroom programming in the school systems, as well as teacher workshops and seminars on the topic. For those who have entered into this personal growth process, the results and impact have been profound. For example, in a number of school systems in Northern California, Seattle, Washington, New York City, New Jersey, and New Haven, the following results have been observed for both elementary and high school students:

Improvements in Positive Social Behavior

- Improved assertiveness
- Better understanding of others
- Better conflict resolution skills
- Improved responsibility
- Better thinking before acting
- Improved frustration tolerance
- Better sharing and cooperative behavior
- Improved positive attachment to family and school
- Improved scores on standardized achievement tests
- Improved caring, compassionate, and empathetic behavior towards others
- Higher self-esteem
- Better social decision making
- More likely to be sought out by others for social engagement and for help

Reduction in Negative Social Behavior

- Less sadness and depression

- Less anxiety and social withdrawal
- Less delinquency
- Less drug use
- Fewer suspensions and expulsions among low-achieving students
- Less aggressiveness and self-destructive behavior
- Less violence in the classroom and elsewhere
- Fewer verbal put-downs
- Less anti-social, self-destructive and socially disordered behavior

Summary

In summary, emotional intelligence and faith are vital factors in our navigational efforts to process daily events and relate effectively to those who enter our personal space.

Success in our daily endeavors depends on our utilizing our emotional intelligence and applying our newly acquired interpersonal skills wisely and consistently. Every day we are challenged to come to the intersection of life where life is at its best, to apply our faith and our emotional intelligence to real life problems and events.

First, take ten to twelve minutes and assess your own level of emotional intelligence by completing the forms in Appendix A, B and C. This will tell you the areas you need to strengthen and the areas in which you already have strength. Using this book and other resources, start the process of enhancing your faith and emotional intelligence skill so they are ready as circumstances and situations arise in your daily walk.

Your study of emotional intelligence through the use of this book will help you learn:

- To understand why people act as they do
- To determine your current level of emotional intelligence
- To diffuse conflicts and tense situations
- To improve your relationships
- To keep your emotions in check and help others do so also
- To work or study more efficiently and productively
- To increase your confidence and social grace

Come on along into the world where faith and emotional intelligence intersect . . . . *LIVING LIFE @ ITS BEST.*

PART I

THE PERSONAL ADJUSTMENT TRAITS OF EMOTIONAL INTELLIGENCE

People who are emotionally intelligent know who they are, the purpose for which they live, and what they can become. It starts from within each individual. We call these the *personal adjustment traits* that make up each of us as individuals. Yet, each individual is uniquely different. Each person's meaning is based on the premise that God created each person in his image and for his purpose when he breathed into them the breath of life. Each person is to live fully as God intended.

The *personal adjustment* traits of emotional intelligence are comprised of Self-Respect, Self-Awareness, Assertiveness, Independence and Self-Actualization. Together these five traits reflect the personal and inner strength of an individual's make-up. The reflection of each person's personal and inner strength is dependent on the degree to which the configuration or pattern of these five areas have developed into maturity and fullness.

Being insightful and honest about oneself is the hallmark of a well functioning individual. Being well grounded and expressive in each of the various personal components is foundational to living an effective life in one's vocation, marriage and social relationships. Being committed and confident in one's faith in God, is basic to living life fully and abundantly. Acquiring the skill of living out the personal adjustment traits of emotional intelligence is the starting point for living effectively as a fulfilled person and as a person of influence.

SELF-RESPECT . . . .

Through the Strategic Actions of Naaman's Servant Girl

THE UNWRAPPING OF SELF-RESPECT

Ever meet someone that regarded themselves more highly than they ought? We would declare them to be prideful or arrogant. We would think that the possibility of humility is not in them. At times, we have all felt that way, and we have had to deal with someone who considers themselves "too big for their own britches."

Self-respect is another term for self-esteem or self-regard. It involves appropriate and honest thinking of oneself. It refers to the understanding and appreciation for the implications of one's own thoughts, emotions, and behaviors. It is our task to identify and name our thoughts, feelings, and actions that emerge and of which we become aware. This awareness is the unique duty of each person every day. Feelings, for example, are not to be ignored or dismissed, but accepted as part of our personality. We are to engage our thoughts, feelings, and behavior by bringing them under conscious control. The goal is to admit, accept, and manage our feelings, not deny or suppress them. The same goes for our thoughts and behavior patterns.

Self-respect is also known to be our internal sense of our personal and social bearings. It's the external presentation we make to others that conveys our sense of self-confidence and self-worth. Much of our social effectiveness is determined by the way we present our self and project our self-worth. We are more effective if we think well of our self and reflect it when interacting with others. It is like presenting our self well to the business community when seeking employment.

Our self-respect is not a fixed characteristic or viewpoint. It can go up or down over time. That is why we need to keep assessing our self throughout the day and over time. We determine that we are very good or less than good depending on the way we deal with our circumstances at the time. This is an ongoing process by which we are filled with hope at one time but may then be driven to the edge of self-depreciation at another time.

Finally, self-respect is learned. It forms from our history of thinking patterns, feelings patterns and behavioral patterns. If we have had a series of successful experiences, we tend to think well of our self. We can also affect the self-respect of others. We can contribute to the self-respect and esteem of others, or we can denigrate others by how we act towards them and convey our thoughts and feelings about them.

SELF-RESPECT AMPLIFIED BY
THE SERVANT GIRL OF NAAMAN

Whenever the concept of self-respect is considered, we usually turn our attention to examples from the military, particularly the officers within the military. This was as true in Biblical days as it is today. Somehow, military officers seem to come pre-trained before enrolling in the military and have their self-respect well established. They seem to refine it through their military training and exercises. Their experience in combat and other war maneuvers refines it even further. It appears that greater self respect and self-esteem positively correlates with years of service, rank and combat experience.

Naaman was no exception. He was the Commander-in-Chief of the Syrian military. He had been to battle on numerous occasions and had established a stunning winning record. He was considered as one of the top military strategists and military leaders of all time. He had cause to be self-respecting and to value himself, his knowledge, and his skills with high regard. He spoke with command and confidence in his voice. His sense of self-worth was reinforced by his own military troops who revered him. The King of Syria definitely regarded him highly. This gave him even more reason to regard himself well.

However, despite his military record and leadership heritage, Naaman had an area of weakness and vulnerability. He had an area of his life about which he was keenly self-conscious. No doubt he often privately complained about this problem. It was an area of concern that dominated his thinking when he was not in uniform or in an active military mode. In contrast, the inadequacy or shame that he felt was overcome when he went into a military mode or into battle. Perhaps his dominant role in the military and his winning record helped him compensate for the dreaded disease of all time, leprosy.

Naaman was a rich, famous and well-traveled man. He probably had access to whatever medical care was available and whatever home remedies could be concocted as a hopeful cure. Yet, a cure was not in sight. He had to live with leprosy despite his desire to hide when not in his military mode. Feelings of helplessness and depression were his plight. Perhaps he even had periodic self-defeating thoughts of bringing his life to a close. Some days were tough, hard to live and survive.

In the midst of his emotional and medical struggles, Naaman was destined to have a defining moment, a turning point. A new servant girl came to live within his household. She became the answer to his dilemma. Unfortunately, she remains un-named in Scripture. With her new employment in Naaman's home, his life was about to change and take a new direction for evermore. His self-respect and self-regard was about to be turned around and enhanced. It took time, however.

The servant girl lived within his household for a number of years. She was a very meek, quiet and lowly servant girl. She was a displaced person from Israel. Her formal assignment was to be the handmaiden for Naaman's wife. However, she was a woman with positive personal characteristics, physical appearance, and abilities. She had a special concern for her master, Naaman. She had a sense of compassion, empathy, and soon developed a desire to help solve his chronic health problem. After all, a servant's purpose in life was to meet the needs of their master.

She went to her mistress, Naaman's wife, and confided an idea to her that might be worthy of Naaman's consideration. She proceeded to spell out a plan for Naaman to visit a prophet in Samaria where she had been raised as a child. She knew the prophet's abilities and powers and thought he could heal Naaman. Although a bold idea, she had the self-respect to suggest it for Naaman. From that point onward, we no longer learn anything more about the servant girl. She fades from history. Task accomplished!

As the story further unfolds, Naaman agreed to the plan and told his king what the servant girl had said. The king agreed that Naaman should go to Israel and also wrote a letter of introduction to the King of Israel, sending it along with massive gifts. The King of Israel was furious at the thought of his plight to aid in healing Naaman of leprosy, but Elisha, the prophet, came to his rescue. The prophet told Naaman to go to the pool of Siloam and dip into it seven times. He was to exercise faith in so doing. To a military man that must have seemed ridiculous. Naaman refused, but his servant convinced him to try it, as he had nothing to lose. Naaman did, in faith, and was healed of his chronic and debilitating leprosy. He must have been jubilant!

Naaman returned home and followed the word of the Lord from that time onward like he had never done before. Not only did Naaman live a life of obedience and reverence for God, he lived a life of even greater and genuine self-regard and self-respect.

It is possible that Naaman sent a message of gratitude to the servant girl. Her willingness to step forward out of her submissive role as a slave girl allowed her to speak as God's voice for the moment. She represented the defining moment in Naaman's life. Had she known the full story, her own self-esteem and self-regard would have become more clearly defined and enhanced through this event and experience as well.

Don't we all take great satisfaction and personal pride when we are the point person that gives direction to someone struggling and that advice changes their life for evermore? *Dare to be like Naaman's servant to speak at the defining moment in the life of another!*

FURTHER READING ON SELF-RESPECT

II Kings 5
Job 29:21
Isaiah 25:3
I Samuel 24:1-7; 26:7-11
Song of Songs 5:10-16

DISCUSSION QUESTIONS

Self-Respect Discussion Questions

1. What do you do to increase yourself regard or self-respect?

2. How do you as a married couple build into each other positive self regard? How do you build up your children and other family members in their self regard?

3. Have you ever been the "life changer" in the life of another person . . . . an agent of change?

4. Has anyone come into your life and helped you bring about a positive change in direction?

5. Who has been the person of greatest influence on your life? Why?

The Servant Girl Discussion Questions

1. Do you have a need for a caring "servant girl" in your life? How would you acquire such a relationship?

2. In what way can you be a caring "servant girl" in the life of someone who is in need or deserves such a relationship?

3. What do you think of Naaman's response to the advice of the prophet on his behalf? How would you have responded differently than how Naaman responded?

4. Did you notice how the "servant girl" faded out so as not to take the attention or credit from the prophet or God himself?

SELF-RESPECT DAILY EXERCISES

1. Find some way this week to carry out an action for someone that will help them in their time of need.

2. Think about the thoughts and feelings of the "servant girl" in Naaman's life, both before and after his healing. Try to place yourself in her shoes at the time she served Naaman and his household. Feel the anxiety she felt when she struggled to come up with a helpful solution for Naaman.

3. What are some of the ways God has healed or come to the aid of someone you know at their time of need? What about your need at some time in your life?

SELF-RESPECT ARROWHEADS

- The backbiter is like a cat that will lie down and purr after he has eaten the canary.
- Humility could be the soloist of the Thanksgiving Chorus.
- The first thing to do after you have failed is to admit it.
- We are not the way we are because we feel the way we feel, but we feel the way we feel because we are the way we are.
- There is no parachute that will let us down easy when the balloon of pride bursts; neither is there a choice of landing.
- He who has the "big head" is like unto a thumb tack; he makes a big showing but bears little weight.
- You can't be sure unless you are pure.
- The brighter the fire glows, the less smoke it throws.
- He who will not come down from his high horse is generally thrown off.
- Are you the "Jack Horner" who selfishly sticks his thumb into the Christmas pie and says, "What a good boy am I"?
- Some people are actually knocked over with a feather—one feather in their hat and they topple.
- He who speaks proud words must be his own audience.
- 'Tis late to thank after you have been reminded of the neglect.
- The shoe never fits some people's understanding.
- Some men go up with a whiz like a skyrocket but come down like one too—a sooty stick.
- Often times the spots we see on others are but shadows of the stains on your spectacles.
- The Pharisee who thanked God for himself was at least grateful for little.
- Some confess their faults, others caress them.
- Weave your rags of self-righteousness and your warped life into a rag rug and 'twill be easier to keep them under your feet.
- Ingratitude chums around with selfishness and pride.
- Why is it that people who love themselves, so often try to be somebody else?

- Some people thumb their way through life by keeping others under their thumb.
- Do you take pride in being headstrong? The bullhead is a scavenger.
- He who walks on the stilts of self-righteousness finds it difficult to kneel.
- I am no better than my worst.
- 'Tis better to be a glowing than a glaring light.
- Keep yourself balanced and you will have less trouble balancing your books.
- Coasting down the hill of our achievements brings us below the level where we started our climb.
- Mr. I-Told-You-So is the fellow who never lets anyone else tell him.

My Self-Respect Arrowhead _____

MY WEEKLY JOURNAL ON SELF-RESPECT
The *self-respect* lessons I learned this week were....

SELF-AWARENESS . . . .
Through the Emotional Expressions of David

THE UNWRAPPING OF SELF-AWARENESS

Being aware and alert of what is going on around you is wise in today's world. Our world is fraught with anger, competitiveness, selfishness, and combativeness. Thus, everyone needs to be aware of their surroundings and be prepared to act defensively.

Likewise, we need to be keenly aware of our own emotions. Emotions drive much of our behavior. We act out of our own fear, anxiety and doubt, as well as our pride, joy, confidence and happiness. Similarly, we react or respond to such feelings and emotions in others. Unfortunately, we are more emotion driven than rational driven. The wise mind is generally played down in our decision making and choice of action alternatives.

The ability to understand others, to be open to diversity, read non-verbal cues, actively listen, and look at life from the perspective of other people encompasses the essential elements of self-awareness. This is an important component of emotional intelligence. It is what brings two people together so they can have a bonding experience or intimacy. It is what keeps people together and prevents the all too frequent interpersonal divides marital divorce, church splits, personal breakdowns, and corporate buyouts.

Further, self-awareness is the ability to appraise, manage and effectively utilize emotionally charged information. It is the ability to understand our own emotions, manage our emotions and use our emotions wisely and adaptively in everyday problem solving. Likewise, it is identifying the emotions of others and managing the emotions expressed by others. This may include strategies and techniques to elevate negative and self-defeating moods or moderate overly positive moods. It is akin to the old adage of "walking in the moccasins of another person." Lastly, emotional self-awareness includes the mutual communication of how one feels, so that desired outcomes can be achieved for the mutual good of all concerned.

For example, in the work environment, emotions affect how managers and employers make decisions, plan for the future, solve problems, innovate programs, and interact with customers and vendors. The employees with the most emotional assets to a company are those who manage their emotions to enhance their performance and the performance of others in all work related processes. On the other hand, employees whose emotions are not well understood and not well managed, degrade themselves and others and ultimately their work performance. This can cost a company or an organization the loss of huge sums of money, time, as well as personal and physical resources.

SELF-AWARENESS AMPLIFIED BY DAVID

There is no greater demonstration of authentic feelings being expressed than when "Jesus wept" over the death and burial of his friend Lazarus. No doubt, Jesus was very aware of his feelings and the feelings of the family and the gathered friends (John 11:38). When Jesus cried over the City of Jerusalem, he again displayed his strong and deep feelings of loss and grief (Luke 19:41).

Indeed, crying is a strong emotional expression that indicates the presence of a deep and distressing feeling. Crying helps to bring the feeling to our attention and consciousness, as well as to other people. Peter wept bitterly as the events of Christ's death unfolded (Matthew 26:75). There were others known for authentic emotional expressions. Nehemiah demonstrated his emotional attachment to the city when he wept over its destroyed condition (Nehemiah 1:4). And John wept deeply when no one was found to open the scrolls and read them. (Revelation 5:4). Deep feelings create the need to cry.

A strong and exemplary man who captures our attention because of his readiness to express his feelings openly and publicly was David. We know David as having been described as "a man after God's own heart," an emotional reference in itself. David cried on many occasions. David fasted and wept for over two weeks for his dying child (II Samuel 12:15-24).

David wept the most between Saul and himself. A number of examples show his deep emotional expressions. David wept at the destruction of Ziklag (I Samuel 30:4). David wept with Jonathan before fleeing Saul's wrath (I Samuel 20:41). He wept over Saul's and Jonathan's deaths (II Samuel 1:17). He wept over the murders of Abner (II Samuel 3:32) and Amnon (II Samuel 13:36). He wept when his son, Absalom, died (II Samuel 18:33). He wept over his own sinful behavior (Psalm 51:17, Psalm 32:4). David was not a cry baby, but an emotional man with the ability and freedom to express his feelings.

We cry when there is loss of a personal relationship and the associated loss of support, companionship, encouragement and good will. David is an excellent example of a man who formed deep personal and long-term relationships with a number of men. No wonder he cried at the time of their death. David was not the only one who cried at such occasions. Many others cried, many of whom were men. A review of the incidences in which men wept throughout scripture illustrates the deep relationships that men are able to form with others. The times in which men express themselves are usually when a friend becomes a victim of crime, jealously, illness or death.

It is well known that those who experience significant loss, such as the death of a loved one process that loss in a systematic and sequential manner. This process is called grief. First, there is the *shock and disbelief* of the news. Secondly, *anger* emerges as we come to realize the loss and how it came about. Thirdly, there is *bargaining with God* in our attempt to reverse the news and bring back the person or minimize the impact of the death. Fourthly, *depression* is experienced as we focus our attention on the permanent absence of the person and the nature of the relationship that existed prior to the loss. Lastly, there is a time of *recovery and rehabilitation.* That is when we come to know that we can survive and live beyond and without the person we loved so dearly. The pattern of David's weeping in the various situations he faced, unfolded all the elements of the grieving process.

Feelings of joy and happiness also were true of David. The many psalms that David wrote depict the full range of his feelings, such as joy, sorrow, disappointment, and thankfulness. David was not only an emotional man who was strong and independent enough to express his emotions, but he often expressed them publicly. He was also a brave man who knew what fear was all about. We all remember David standing at the side of the brook and looking at the big man Goliath face to face. We all grew up singing the song which expresses one of David's greatest life events:

> Only a boy named David
> Only a rippling brook
> Only a boy named David
> and five little stones he took.
> One little stone went into the sling
> and the sling went round and round.
> Round and round and round it went.
> One little stone went up in the air
> and the giant came tumbling down.

No doubt, after the giant fell to the ground there was within David and the army he represented great celebration with feelings of joy, exhilaration, happiness and relief. These are all strong emotions of every person.

However, while the song speaks of David's bravery and skill, we can also imagine that within him was a sense of fear, one of the strongest emotions of mankind. While fear usually propels us into action, it can also immobilize and debilitate us, but Christ gave the clear command to "fear not". God gave David command over his fear countless times. *Dare to have the emotional expressions like David at critical times of trauma and loss!*

FURTHER READING ON SELF-AWARENESS

I and II Samuel
Genesis 48:17-20
Jonah 3:10
Luke 10:23-24
John 1:29-31
2 Corinthians 7:10-13

DISCUSSION QUESTIONS

Self-Awareness Discussion Questions

1. Why is emotional self-awareness so important to our relationships? To our work? To our state of happiness?

2. What do you do to improve your self-awareness? How do you help your children become more emotionally self-aware?

3. How can you become more emotionally aware in all your relationships and lifestyle?

4. Do you know anyone who is a good example of emotional self-awareness? How are they a good example for you? Tell how you try to learn from them or imitate their lifestyle.

David Discussion Questions

1. Read more about David this week from I and II Samuel and the other references noted above.

2. What are the qualities of David as young man that you admire?

3. Share your history of strong emotional expressions like David. How have you been similar or different from David?

4. What causes David to be a good example of emotional self-awareness?

5. How do you understand and reconcile the fearless David with the crying David?

6. What else do you know of David that adds to your understanding of him as a good example or model on which to base your life? Tell the story in a way that would encourage others to use David as a model for their life.

SELF-AWARENESS DAILY EXERCISES

1. Look around you all week and find a few examples of people living a life based on emotional self-awareness. Write a brief summary of what you observed. Share it with others during the week.

2. Do an acrostic on SELF-AWARENESS bringing out the meaning of the concept.

3. Compose a poem or song about David, telling of his virtues as a young leader.

SELF-AWARENESS ARROWHEADS

- People who are "down in the mouth" have the V for Victory turned upside down.
- Revenge is meaner than the injury.
- He that weepeth not, reapeth not.
- You will have your ups and downs on the Ferris-wheel of emotionalism.
- The same sunshine which inspires exclamations of joy becomes unbearable after two weeks without a cloud.
- We are not the way we are because we feel the way we feel, but we feel the way we feel because we are the way we are.
- Anger, like the avalanche, blazes a trail which it never again uses.
- The more you lose of a temper, the more you have.
- A tear stain is the best bookmark you can leave in a Bible.
- If you live in fear of death you will die in fear of life.
- "I" is always in the center of anxiety.
- People that have no feeling will change very little when they die.
- Jesus said, "Take heed therefore how ye hear," knowing that the equilibrium is in the ear.
- Some confess their faults, others caress them.
- Anger, like the avalanche, blazes a trail which it never again uses.
- You are framed for judgment in your ugliest pose.

- The sun sets early for those who live in the valley.

My Self-Awareness Arrowhead _____

MY WEEKLY JOURNAL OF SELF-AWARENESS

The *self-awareness* lessons I learned this week were....

ASSERTIVE COMMUNICATION . . . .

Through the Timely Assertive Voice of Esther

THE UNWRAPPING OF ASSERTIVE COMMUNICATION

All people have worth, inherent dignity and the right of respect. All people have the right to intentionally represent their feelings, ideas, preferences and desires. All people also have the right to engage in appropriate verbal expressions designed to convey their needs, interests and desires to others. And, finally, all people must grant freedom to others to appropriately express their beliefs, feelings, desires and needs. In all communication, people desire to be spoken to with respect and consideration. These are the essential principles of assertiveness.

Specific action-steps to implement a preferred course of action or to achieve a particular outcome are inherent in all assertive communication interchanges. Assertiveness involves both an intentional action plan to bring about some particular positive experience and/or intentionally terminate an unwanted or unpleasant experience to which one is being subjected.

Assertive communication is best understood in the context of the two extreme positions, *passivity* and *aggressiveness.* It is generally inappropriate to be silent, withholding, unforthcoming and passive in situations in which one desires to achieve something. Likewise, it is generally considered undesirable to be pushy, bullish, dominant, intolerant, disobedient, combative, or aggressive to get one's way. To be assertive, one has to find the balance point between being passive and being aggressive. While assertive communication skills are generally preferred and needed, there are times when a more passive or a more aggressive approach is appropriate and necessary. It is important to know which style of behavior to express and when to express it.

Specifically, some examples of assertive communication skills would involve the initiation of conversation, raising a hand to obtain permission to speak or act, saying "no" when something is wrong, voicing an opinion, asking for help, and sharing personal views. Assertiveness always involves the balance between the meeting of one's own needs and a respect for other people's need and their preferences. It could be said that being well spoken is the balance point between being outspoken and being unspoken.

Assertiveness is not only appropriate and effective verbalization, but it also involves the process of active listening. We respect the rights and needs of others as we take time to listen to them. Active listening involves making eye contact, screening out competing distractions, nodding and verbally acknowledging what the other person has just stated. It may or may not involve full agreement to what is being said.

Active listening is important as it acknowledges that we all have a need to feel recognized. It is a way for us to know that we are cared about and respected. Active listening indicates that we care and desire to respect the other person. It is a foundational way of learning about other people, places and things. Listening is the basis on which we make decisions about our future relationship with people.

In summary, assertive communication is best understood in the context of a continuous line. At one end of the spectrum is passivity and at the other end is aggressiveness. Assertiveness is in the middle. *Passive* individuals tend not to express their individual needs or interests being met. They depend upon others to anticipate their needs and meet them. They do not take action to eliminate or stop unpleasant events from taking place in their lives. They are subject to the whims of others and the environment in which they live. On the other hand, *aggressive* people disregard the feelings and rights of others and impose their preferences upon them. They are generally insensitive to people's feelings and to how their actions may impact others. They force their way. They make things happen, often at the great expense of those involved. In contrast, *assertive* people act and speak in a manner that represents their own desires, needs, thoughts and beliefs while being sensitive to the feelings, status and rights of others. Assertive people are generally thoughtful and caring as they interact with others.

ASSERTIVE COMMUNICATION AMPLIFIED BY ESTHER

Queen Esther was not naturally or particularly assertive. Orphaned as an infant, Esther had not been given the opportunity to enjoy a positive and strong beginning in life. She lived between 538 B.C. and 473 B.C. Esther knew hardship. She lived during the years when the Hebrews were taken from their homeland and exiled in Persia. Her birth name was Hadassah, but changed to Esther when exiled and adopted by Mordecai, her uncle. He did not want to call attention to her Jewishness. Her given name, Esther, means "star" in Persian.

She presented herself as a person of low assertiveness and passivity, consistent with the times and culture in which she was reared. Her voice quality was pleasing to the ear. At times, she gave the appearance of confidence even though she may not have felt it at the time. Possibly, as a result of the circumstances surrounding her upbringing, her confidence level became dependent upon her attractiveness and beauty. Mordecai raised her to be a lovely woman in all areas. Mordecai also instructed her to tell no one that she was a Jew. Perhaps she had a deep sense of not belonging to any culture.

The life of Esther was changed when King Ahasuerus of Persia was in the process of seeking a new queen. He had divorced Vashti, his former wife, because she was too oppositional and confrontive. At the King's command, Vashti refused to wear her crown and walk in front of the king's party of inebriated guests to display her physical beauty. Ahasuerus was angered at the insubordination of his wife. The queen had to leave. He ordered her out. The king then put out a call for all of the most beautiful unmarried women in the vast land of Persia to be brought to him.

Of all the women brought to the royal harem to be presented to King Ahasuerus, Esther was thought to be the most likely to chosen, and she was given special attention by the attendants. Indeed, she was subsequently chosen by King Ahasuerus to become queen. Instantaneously, Esther's life came out of obscurity, and it was placed on the fast track of success, notoriety and nobility.

By this time Mordecai had become a government official. He discovered an assassination plot against the king and passed on the information to Queen Esther who then told the king and credited Mordecai for the information. Soon after, Haman was appointed prime minister. Unknown to Esther, an ominous plot began to brew at that time. Haman was planning to have all the Jews in the entire kingdom executed, a plot motivated by a grudge that Haman held against Mordecai. Esther was an innocent party to this historical grudge, but she was about to play a significant role in its resolution. The fact that she was a Jewess was not known to Haman. Haman was taken up by her beauty, not her heritage, just as the king had been.

It wasn't long before Mordecai and the Jews in the empire became aware of the plot to kill them. There was great mourning throughout the kingdom. Esther's attendant was sent to Mordecai to discover the reason for the mourning. Mordecai informed the attendant and asked him to inform Esther. Mordecai pleaded with Esther to save her people by making a personal appeal to the king on behalf of the Jewish people. This placed her in a difficult situation. Her assertive skills and confidence were on the line; as she had not been with the king for over a month would he even see her?

Mordecai's request was not a small one, indeed. Displaced from her own country, family and culture, it was not an easy task for Esther to undertake. Though she was the king's wife and queen, Esther knew that to present herself before the king and reveal that she was a Jewess would be a great risk in itself. She was aware that the king's former wife's aggressive refusal to not parade herself in front of a host of men caused her to lose her marriage. Should Esther displease the king, she could also be divorced, even executed. However, she knew from talking with Mordecai, that risking her life was a choice she had to make if the Jewish people were to be saved. Mordecai reasoned, "Who can say that God has brought you into the palace for just such a time as this?"

Esther became acutely aware that she was in a particular place at a particular time in history. Her natural tendency to be hesitant and passive had to be conquered and an assertive pattern of behavior had to emerge quickly. Further, it had to be convincing in attitude and presentation. It was her time in history to become focused and purpose driven. It was truly Esther's assertive choice-point in life. To go forward with the challenge and assertively give her request to King Ahasuerus was her only choice, but she faced personal risks in the process.

To wither, withdraw or shirk from this challenge would have been cowardly and a total act of passivity. She must have kept telling herself over and over that she became queen to save the Jewish people. Quickly she came to realize that her life had an ultimate purpose. Her plan began by involving her people to fast for three days, and then she would go see the king. "If I perish, I perish," she reasoned. Esther forthrightly and assertively donned her royal robes and approached the king. The king held out his royal scepter to her, signifying that she could proceed to speak to him with her important message. But before doing so, Esther hosted a banquet to which she invited the king and Haman. After a lovely dinner, she invited them both to come back again to a banquet the next day. It was then that Esther delivered her message in an assertive and positive manner asking the king to save her life and the lives of her people. Upon questioning, the king came to realize the wretched death plot of Haman, and Haman was doomed to execution. It was the learned assertive skills of God's chosen servant at a given time in history that turned the events of the world upside down. It was Esther's finest hour.

Upon Esther's request, the king gave her the authority to reverse the edict given by Haman, thus saving the lives of all her people. Esther represents the clear principle that when we stand up and speak out assertively for righteousness, God can use us to bring help to others. We do not know when our finest hour will come. But, may we be ready to stand for the lonely, the hurting, the frightened, the threatened and the disillusioned. *Dare to be a timely assertive voice like Esther at times of historical and critical importance!*

FURTHER READING ON ASSERTIVE COMMUNICATION

Esther 4-10
Exodus 32:31-32
Psalm 51:1-7
Luke 11:5-13

DISCUSSION QUESTIONS

Assertive Communication Discussions Questions

1. What has been your experience in speaking assertively to accomplish a goal?

2. Was it an anxious experience?

3. How do you rate yourself in assertiveness on a scale of 1 – 10 (10 being the highest)?

4. What was your "finest hour" in taking assertive action on behalf of someone? Share your story.

5. Have you ever been faced with a difficult situation you had to address? Did you address it or avoid facing it? How did it go? How do you now look back on it? What would you have done differently?

6. Have you been raised in a home that encouraged assertive communication? If not, how did you go about learning to be assertive so you can be more prepared for any time a situation requiring assertive communication occurs?

Esther Discussion Questions

1. Have you ever been given an assignment to carry out and were not ready to do so, but had to be trained and/or encouraged as Esther in assertiveness?

2. Have you ever had a Mordecai in your life?

3. What is your "take home" lesson based on the life of Esther?

4. How do you know that God has a purpose for your life and that he will be there to lead you, enable you, and protect you as you act to fulfill your purpose?

5. Has this message and illustration of Esther been helpful to you as you now look forward to a similar situation you are now facing? Tell your story and ask others to give you suggestions on how to handle it.

6. Have you ever had an "Esther experience" of a wrong brought to your attention? Share your story of dealing with this.

ASSERTIVE COMMUNICATION DAILY EXERCISES

1. Practice being more assertive each day this week. Note how you have improved by the end of the week.

2. Pay particular attention to assertive people this week so you can learn to be more assertive by watching and imitating them.

3. Pursue the opportunity to speak to or address someone of a higher rank or status than you this week and do so assertively.

ASSERTIVE COMMUNICATION ARROWHEADS

- Some confess their faults, others caress them.
- People who ruthlessly elbow their way through soon discover that the crazy bone is more delicate than the rib.
- An open mouth will soon empty the wisest head.
- E'en though our shadow mimics us in walk, 'Tis good for many that he cannot talk.
- The boaster, like the blower on the threshing machine, gives out only straw and chaff.
- Love is our best defense.

- Heated arguments do not warm the fireside.
- You have said too much when you have said all that can be said.
- 'Tis too much tact, which ne'er doth act.
- Kindness to others, like sunshine on a garden, brings out a rose where you think only thorns could grow.
- Most of our fears are only scarecrows.
- Do not fear the shadows for they merely prove the existence and nearness of light.
- Truth and humility go hand in hand from the scene of an argument.
- The two greatest preachers of all time started out with the word REPENT.
- Big boasters—poor boosters.
- Give and you'll never need to give in.
- You can't determine the "face value" of a gossiper until you have turned your back.
- You come out second best if you try to sit on a porcupine or a sharp tongue.
- Heated arguments do not warm the fireside.
- The fastest runner is apt to have the biggest mouth.
- Embrace convenience and it will run a dagger into your heart.
- Whisper a lie; they'll believe every word; Shout out a truth and they'll say, "It's absurd".
- No one is attracted to an open box or an open mouth.
- There is no tax on the air which we inhale, but there is often a heavy tax on that which we exhale.
- Idle words become the busiest little imps ever set in motion.
- The boaster is like a shallow river with a big mouth.
- Better save your thunder if it is not preceded by a flash.
- A secret, like a clam, tightens up when you pry at it, but opens up if you leave it alone.
- Keep a cool head and you will not get cold feet.
- An open mouth will soon empty the wisest head.

My Assertive Communication Arrowhead _____

MY WEEKLY JOURNAL OF ASSERTIVE COMMUNICATION

The *assertive communication* lessons I learned this week were....

INDEPENDENCE . . . .
Through the Risky Choices of Daniel and Friends

THE UNWRAPPING OF INDEPENDENCE

Human nature cries out for independence! To be tied down and restricted is contrary to the human mind. Adolescent youths are most intent on becoming independent, even before they are ready. However, older adults find it difficult to release their independence, even when they are in need of a care provider overseeing their comings and goings. Independence is the golden ring of human nature.

Independence relates to one's capability of thinking, working and making decisions without the assistance of someone else. Although consultation with others is important and helpful, the ultimate and primary decision-making of independent people is done by the individual person. Independence is also based on one's ability to express thoughts and feelings effectively and the ability to explain concepts clearly to persuade others with ideas and vision.

Independence is a status that we all seek, especially after adolescence. Independence essentially is the ability to be responsible for oneself and make wise choices and decisions in the best interests of oneself, as well as of those important to us and dependent on us. Thus, making good independent decisions must include analyzing the facts and making wise judgments and choices. Independence ideally represents good decision making relative to the options available at the time and under the circumstances in which one finds oneself. Lastly, independence is usually associated with an active conscientious lifestyle, physically, mentally and spiritually. Interestingly, such people tend to live two to three years longer than those who live with a lower level of physical, mental, and spiritual activity.

INDEPENDENCE AMPLIFIED BY DANIEL AND FRIENDS

Many of us have cut our eyeteeth on simple childhood songs and hymns which tell of the basic biblical stories. One of the well-known songs of childhood goes like this:

> Dare to be a Daniel,
> Dare to stand-alone!
> Dare to have a purpose firm!
> Dare to make it known.

The writings of Daniel took place sometime between 605 B.C. and 539 B.C., or perhaps shortly thereafter. Daniel attempted to encourage the exiled Jews by reminding them of God's sovereign plan for Israel during and after the Gentile domination. Some refer to this time as the "Times of the Gentiles." This is when the Babylonian time period began under the ruling domination of King Nebuchadnezzar in Babylon. To be sure, Israel suffered during this period of time, but it was not the end of the story because God is sovereign, as Daniel strongly reminded the Israelites time and time again.

During this time period, King Nebuchadnezzar engaged in three invasions into neighboring Judah taking captives from Judah into Babylon. On the first invasion, Daniel and three of his companions, Hananiah, Misha-el, and Azariah were among the Jewish youths taken into captivity. All four of these men were intelligent and enterprising. They were bold and well educated. They and other promising young men were placed in a special three year training program to become advisors to the Court of King Nebuchadnezzar.

The king deliberately attempted to change their identity from Jewish to Babylonian Gentiles. Daniel and his three friends had their names changed from their original Jewish names to Belteshazzar, Shadrach, Meshach, and Abednego for "political" purposes. The king's food was to become their diet. However, Daniel and his three friends rose to the occasion. They were not passive. They were not aggressive. They were assertive, independent thinkers and men who stood alone as well as together. They proceeded to prove to the steward that their Jewish food was superior to the diet of the Babylonians. Basically, they took a stand against the king's pagan food that was offered to the pagan gods. The king recognized their independence, wisdom and knowledge and looked favorably upon them when their training came to an end. Thus, he then put them on his regular staff of advisors.

As life continued for Daniel and his three friends, they were presented with several additional tests and challenges to prove that the God whom they worshiped was in control. The second test was when the king had a disturbing nightmare of a great statue. When he awoke he could not remember the dream, so none of his advisors could interpret the dream. Therefore, all his advisors were to be executed. In a moment prior to execution, Daniel said he would interpret the dream. God told Daniel what the king had dreamed, and David praised God for the vision and its understanding. He stepped forward and credited God who gave him the dream and the future told in it. By God's grace and empowerment he was able to foretell the dream interpretation that God's will and sovereignty would rise up and then dispose four Gentile empires. Afterwards a kingdom indestructible would remain. Again, Daniel stood alone and stood out in the crowd around the king and captured the attention and admiration of the king. His ability to stand independently with trust in God, at a time of natural crisis, caused him to be promoted to Chief Magistrate of Babylon.

A third challenge grew out of Daniel's interpretation of the king's disturbing dream. Based on the dream and its interpretation, King Nebuchadnezzar erected a golden image and then demanded that all the people bow down to it. Once again, Daniel's friends, Meshach, Shadrach and Abednego stood their ground independently and mutually. They refused to bow down to the golden image. They stood by their faith and their dedication to God alone. This infuriated King Nebuchadnezzar and the three were thrown into the blazing furnace as the edict had decreed.

As the story unfolds, the assertive independence of these three men, while acknowledging their spiritual dependence on God, caught the attention of the king and his entire court. In the depths of the fiery furnace, the three tied men stood erect and then walked about unbound and unsinged, joined by an unidentified fourth person. They stood for their faith in God and God's power. Again, they were protected by the God whom they worshiped and consistently represented to the king during their time of exile. King Nebuchadnezzar blessed the God of Shadrach, Meshach and Abednego and promoted the men to higher positions.

Daniel was called to stand alone for another dream of the king. After the king's description of the dream, Daniel was in anguish to foretell the sad meaning of the king's dream. Daniel stood up independently to tell the king, and he gave all the credit to God. Daniel's prophecy came true after 12 months, and Nebuchadnezzar was chased out of the palace to roam the fields for seven years. Then he was restored as king with great honor, but gave all praise to the King of Heaven!

While the reign of King Nebuchadnezzar came to an end shortly thereafter, Daniel's plight was not over. His dream interpretations kept on, and he was proclaimed 3rd highest ruler in the kingdom. Under King Darius, of the Medes, Daniel was considered for Administrative Officer over the entire empire. The administrators of the 120 provinces plotted against him using his religion. The plan would require everyone to only pray to King Darius. Despite the decree, Daniel continued to pray to his God. The king wanted to save Daniel, but the decree could not be changed. Daniel was thrown into the den of lions for his strong and outspoken independent stand for faith in God alone. Daniel's courageous and forthright faith was rewarded. The mouths of the lions were clamped shut. As a result of Daniel's independent stand of faith in God and God's protection of Daniel, the king learned a lesson about the might of the God of Israel. Not only did the king come to respect Daniel and his God, but decreed, "His God is the living, unchanging God whose kingdom shall never be destroyed and whose power will never come to an end."

Daniel stood tall in the midst of his culture. He stands before us today as a model of an independent spokesperson for God. His independent style of expressing his faith and dependence on God still speaks loud and clear and will for years to come.

Finally, Daniel's message to the king can be our message to the broken world in which we live. God is Sovereign. We are dependent on God for our inner faith and spiritual vitality. We assertively express our faith as we have confidence in our independence from the grip and expectation of our culture. *Dare to be a risk taker, an independent person like Daniel at times of cultural conflict!*

FURTHER READING ON INDEPENDENCE OPTIONS

Daniel 1-9
Psalm 119:45
John 8:31-32, 36
Jeremiah 11:7-8
I Corinthians 9:9-14

DISCUSSION QUESTIONS

Independence Discussion Questions

1. How do you rate yourself on independence using a 10 point scale?

2. How can someone help you become more independent? Who would that person be?

3. Why is independence a trait to be admired and pursued for personal development?

4. In what area of your life could you improve your independence and be more effective personally, socially and spiritually?

Daniel and Friends Discussion Questions

1. Have you ever been in the place in your life similar to that of Daniel and his friends?

2. Which of Daniel's situations look like your situation? Summarize it for someone or the group.

3. Have you sensed God's direction when you were faced with a major predicament? Summarize the situation for someone or the group.

4. How can others help you become more articulate as an independent spokesperson for God? In what types of situations would you like to be a more positive spokesperson for God?

5. Being an independent believer is not easy. How are you doing now? How would you wish to be stronger as an independent believer? What do you need to do to make yourself more independent in your faith and outreach?

6. Do you know of a modern day hero for the faith, such as Daniel? Who would you pick? Could you be that person?

7. How does the life of Daniel encourage your desire for independence in your faith walk?

INDEPENDENCE DAILY EXERCISES

1. Plan and undertake one "witnessing" event this week all by yourself. First, discuss it with someone as a coach, but carry it out by yourself

2. Think of something someone else could do for the name of Christ, and then serve as a coach and cheerleader for them.

3. Imagine acting alone while carrying out an activity that would be a witness for God's power and presence in this world.

INDEPENDENCE ARROWHEADS

- A fool is swallowed up by his own mouth.
- Use your head when the load is too heavy for your hands.
- We all scratch the gears occasionally when we start shifting for ourselves.
- Too many have chosen myopia as their Utopia.
- Prayer is breaking down our unwillingness, not God's.
- He who eyes the walk of others stubs his own toe.
- A baby finds it natural to shake his head but learns with difficulty to nod it.
- He who at the fork tries to take both roads will soon find his legs too short.
- Plow and you will be treading a path that no one else has trod.
- As the window is balanced by the hidden weight, so is a man balanced by convictions within.

- Lost sheep may think there is no danger, but they are only pulling the wool over their own eyes.
- A free-thinker is a slave in action.
- It is selfish to worry about the chickens coming home to roost and not to think of the damage they do while out.
- Why is it that people who love themselves, so often try to be somebody else?
- A dictator is one who rules everyone but himself.
- Some bracelets turn out to be handcuffs.
- A weak foundation—a house full of cracks.
- He who does no more than he must will soon show signs of rust.
- Make hay while the sun shines, but grow it when it rains.

My Independence Arrowhead _____

MY WEEKLY JOURNAL OF INDEPENDENCE

The *independence* lessons I learned this week were....

SELF-ACTUALIZATION . . . .
Through the Confident Courage of Jabez

THE UNWRAPPING OF SELF-ACTUALIZATION

Peak experiences are rare. Few of us know what peak experience feelings are like. Just what is it like to feel totally fulfilled and exhilarated? What are the inner feelings when we have successfully completed a task totally beyond our imagination, expectation and prior experiences?

Self-actualization is the experience of feeling totally fulfilled. It's living at the peak of one's capability and potential. However, before self-actualization can be achieved, the basic needs of life must be met. It is then developmentally and progressively experienced as we devote concentrated time and energy to the enjoyment of our preferred leisure activities, the focused pursuit of our long term educational and social interests, the full development of our mind and body, the cheerful giving of our personal resources to a worthy cause, and the free engagement in the growth and expression of our faith. It is the combination of these factors that brings about self-actualization, not just one of them.

It is in the extraordinary that self-actualization occurs. Self-actualization is attained as we are free to live a life beyond the ordinary; a life that makes a significant difference in the global world. Finally, self-actualization is achieved as we base our lives and choices on biblical principles and live fully for God's glory. John Haggai, founder of the Haggai Institute, said it best, "Believe in something so big that it will fail unless God is in it."

However, before self-actualization can be realized, it is vital that fear be resolved and brought under control, especially social fear. Fear squelches and limits one's lifestyle and expressions. Fear inhibits. It causes us to hold back in many or all areas of our life. Once fear is brought under control, freedom prevails. Only then can one pursue a life style of learning, open expression, and opportunity. Self-actualization can only be pursued and developed when fear is cast out and confidence prevails.

Further, prior to the achievement of self-actualization, and in addition to fear resolution, forgiveness of oneself and others for past wrong doings and hurt is essential. It has been said that forgiveness is as much of a benefit to the person expressing forgiveness as it is to the person receiving forgiveness. Forgiving is the change of one's attitude, perceptions and emotions towards another person. It is the giving-up of the opportunity or chance to engage in retaliatory or revengeful actions.

Forgiveness requires the examination of one's own thinking about another person who caused injury and changes the way we think about and relate to that person in the future. When we forgive, we are in a position to shift our focus from seeing the other person as bad or undesirable, to seeing them as a good person who has done something harmful or wrong. Forgiveness allows us to have the freedom to feel differently and, in time, begin to behave differently towards another. As we move towards self-actualization, we make choices about how to *reflectively respond* rather than to behave *reactively* towards others and various situations. Reflective response patterns are much more healthy and satisfying for all parties. Forgiveness also allows the forgiven party to live a life in pursuit of self-actualization (See Appendix D).

In summary, self-actualization is an active process of being and becoming increasingly inner-directed and integrated at all levels of thinking, feeling, body functioning and spirituality. It is a process of moving from normal living towards growth, development, and the full unfolding of a person's God-given human potential.

SELF-ACTUALIZATION AND THE LIFE OF JABEZ

During the time following the conquest of Canaan by Joshua and during the time of the succession of judges, Jabez was born into the tribe of Judea. He lived during the reign of the judges and King David. He eventually became a notable head of his clan. All this took place when the Promise Land was partitioned into sections of real estate for each of the tribes. He knew the meaning of having a prescribed section of land.

Yet, he felt inhibited, restricted, and limited by this prescribed section of land. Jabez had confidence in himself and knew he could be responsible for more land. He knew that land and territory dictated the fate of people. He also knew the limitations of walls and gates. And he knew that his future, his personal effectiveness and the positioning of his clan would require broader and greater territory. He was eager to reach out for more land and associated responsibility.

Jabez was an honorable man, more honorable than his brothers. Jabez wanted to do more for God and God's Kingdom. While Jabez also was an ordinary man in many ways, he desired to live an extraordinary life. He was in pursuit of self-actualization. He knew that self-actualization does not occur in the confines of limitations, restrictions, inhibitions, or boundaries. It occurs as we are able to break loose and embrace new territory, new opportunities, new developments, and new challenges. Freedom to extend oneself is the essence of self-actualization. He knew that fully.

For Jabez, life started out in trauma. His mother named him Jabez because of the pain she experienced in giving birth to him. The name, Jabez, means pain in Hebrew. The name carries with it the understanding that, "He causes pain." It must have been a very painful birth for his mother to give him a name that carries the remembrance of pain for the rest of her and his life. The pain she experienced must have been beyond the normal pain of childbirth at that time in history. We do not really know if it was only physical pain, emotional pain or both. Probably it was both, and it may have even involved post-partum depression.

Psychological research has long demonstrated that early mild-moderate stress for a newborn strengthens the physical and emotional status of the newborn. On the other hand, severe trauma weakens the potential for full physical and emotional growth of the new-born. The effect of early pain and other early stressful experiences is enduring and carries into the adult years of life. One must then work to overcome the limiting factor and intentionally pursue one's full potential in God's plan. Overcoming limiting factors makes us even more determined and resolute in all areas of life. Self-actualization then becomes a possibility.

We know little about how Jabez was subsequently raised and the events of his early childhood. However, we do know that he desired more opportunity as he approached and attained manhood. He desired more responsibility, more territory and more challenge. His lifestyle indicates he may have been a Type A personality. Such individuals live life as a challenge. They are competitive, determined and purpose driven. They live life non-stop.

As Jabez grew and matured, he became a very sensitive young man. He had feelings for other people. In fact, his two-sentence prayer includes a request of God that he not causes pain to fall on anyone. No doubt, Jabez learned from his home-schooling with his mother about the God of Israel, who freed his forefathers from slavery, rescued them from powerful enemies, established them in a land of plenty and continued to operate in the lives of his people.

Jabez also knew the potential for evil. He seemed to learn that trauma in life can create the negative urges of retaliation, retribution, reprisal and misplaced aggression. In fact, Jabez's prayer included a section in which he asks that he be kept from doing evil. Instead, it was his desire and prayer that he would live a life of self-actualization before his God, his family and before his fellowmen. Eventually, God graciously granted him his extraordinary request! Wow!!!

Here is his prayer as recorded in I Chronicles 4:10, " . . . *Oh, that you would bless me and enlarge my territory! Let your hand be with me, and keep me from harm so that I will be free from pain."* *(NIV)*

Ultimate self-actualization is when God places his hand of blessing on a person's life. Jabez prayed for God's blessing on his life. God responded in his favor. For Jabez like anyone else, life starts out simple, concrete, practical and basic. For Jabez, it started out with a cry of pain. The paths of life mature, shape, and strengthen the individual. They direct and focus the individual. Some people reach the expansion level of life and proceed to live beyond their comfort zone. They move into territories unknown, unexplored and uncharted. By so doing, they begin to enter the world of self-actualization.

May we all pray for greater blessings and greater influence. Self-actualization is ours as we focus on the extraordinary. Life beyond our comfort zone is where self-actualization begins. It also requires living on the edge of the known and unknown. It is experienced by focusing beyond one's inadequacies, deficiencies or impairments.

To be sure, enlarging one's borders may not necessarily be in the form of land. It may be people. It may be business opportunities. It may be enlarging one's social network. It may be one's neighborhood. It may be family or friendships. It may be one's personal impact on others. It may be one's church. It may be one's outreach ministry. Or, it may be one's professional life and contacts.

Jabez was bold enough to ask God for the impossible, for the unknown, for the stretch of his life. It is when the zone of our safety touches the zone of our risk that we begin to experience our potential for self-actualization. Self-actualization is exponential living. It is experiencing the exponential blessings of God. It means leaving the mediocre, the comfortable and the tried and true. It is living in the here and now, while having extraordinary futuristic impact and extraordinary satisfaction. Jabez understood this dual dynamic.

Self-actualization is summed up most fully and succinctly in God's directive, "Be ye holy, because I am holy." (I Peter 1:16, NIV) To be holy and to bring full glory to God, the God in the Highest is the essence of self-actualization. In a practical sense, it is when we become the light of the world and the salt of the earth, that we experience the full joy of our salvation.

Finally, the Apostle Paul understood the concept of self-actualization and had it in focus when he pronounced the strong words, "*I can do everything through him who gives me strength.*" (Philippians 4:13, NIV). Those same strong words speak out to us today as we take daily steps in our pursuit of self-actualization. *Dare to be confident and courageous like Jabez seeking God for an expansive opportunity!*

FURTHER READING ON SELF-ACTUALIZATION

Ecclesiastes 1:16-18; 2:4-11; 3:13; 11:8
I Chronicles 4:9-10
Psalms 103:5
Luke 6:21
John 7:37-39
I Peter 1:8-9
3 John 3-4

DISCUSSION QUESTIONS

Self-Actualization Questions

1. What have you done lately to move towards self-actualization?

2. How do you rate yourself on self-actualization using the scale of 1 – 10 (10 being the highest score)? Has it varied over time?

3. Have you ever had a "Wow" experience? What was it?

4. How do you view yourself living out an exponential influence in your daily life?

Jabez Discussion Questions

1. What do you admire about Jabez? Why?

2. What was the factor that helped Jabez live life fully and in the pursuit of self-actualization?

3. What is your "take home" lesson from Jabez?

4. How do you account for his life of achievement when it started out in pain and limitation?

SELF-ACTUALIZATION DAILY EXERCISES

1. Find someone that you believe has "Jabez" qualities. What are the qualities you admire in that person?

2. Think about the "Jabez" qualities you possess. Are you living them out fully?

3. Do you have an area of fear or a need for forgiveness that you should resolve so you can move forward towards self-actualization and holy living?

SELF-ACTUALIZATION ARROWHEADS

- The climber never loses his balance looking upward.
- The morning-glory always twines toward the right.
- The sunset holds a richer glow for those who have borne the heat of the day.
- Prosperity is around the "U" turn of repentance.
- Mountain-climbing keeps us on our toes.
- Make hay while the sun shines, but grow it when it rains.
- The midnight oil is often better than the noonday sun.
- How can we be heirs of God if we do not accept His will?
- Is prayer only a one-way line or do we listen too?
- The thread finds its way by trusting the needle-eye.
- The brighter the fire glows, the less smoke it throws.
- Idleness is no beauty-rest.
- He that has faith without works or works without faith will get no farther than the fellow pulling on one oar.
- Why brood over such ugly ducklings as worries and fears?
- The head grows smaller and the heart bigger when we pray.
- He who first treads a path directs the steps of generations after him.
- You always have time for the thing you put first.
- There is no better binding for a book than truth.
- We shall miss heaven, if we fail to take lessons from the "little child."
- The way of life is the only road which does not come to a dead end.
- If you would have clear vision, then wash your eyes with tears.
- Plow and you will be treading a path that no one else has trod.
- If our lot in life is a hard one, let us learn from the moss which grows beautiful on the hard, unyielding surface on the rock.
- When God fulfills, He fills full.

- He who will not cross the foothills of menial tasks can never scale the snowcapped peak.
- Safety depends on an internal condition, not on external circumstance.
- God cannot wield until we yield.
- Our best adds beauty even to our failures.
- We should be on top of the mountain rather than allow the mountain to be on top of us.
- Gratitude generally gets us a second helping.
- The shoes of the "preparation of the Gospel of peace" do not blister.
- 'Tis the work we do after the whistle blows that gives us the promotion.

My Self-Actualization Arrowhead _____

MY DAILY JOURNAL ON
SELF-ACTUALIZATION

The *self-actualization* lessons I learned this week were....

PART II

THE INTERPERSONAL TRAITS OF EMOTIONAL INTELLIGENCE

People who are highly effective in their interpersonal and social relationships are prepared and ready to express themselves with ease, and are able to connect with the emotional state of others. The three components that make up the *interpersonal traits* of emotionally intelligent individuals are Empathy, Social Responsibility and Interpersonal Bonding. The stronger each of these three components is developed and manifested, the better a person's interaction and bond with others. Our social world, in general, is better navigated as our interpersonal skills and abilities are well honed.

Most of our interpersonal contacts go reasonably well. Overall, we are in a win-win situation with most people. However, we do have some relationships that are of a losing nature. In most relationships, we stay connected over time, whether or not things go our way. Stronger bonds with others develop a sense of trust, loyalty and greater leadership influence.

There are times, however, when we lack confidence or do not have the necessary experience or skill to effectively navigate a particular social situation that we encounter. We do the best we can. However, as we improve in the three interpersonal traits of empathy, social responsibility and interpersonal bonding, we increase our footprint of general influence and social impact. As we demonstrate increasing strength in each of the three components or in some combination of these three components, our social functioning and personal impact improves and broadens.

EMPATHETIC
INTERACTIONS . . . .

Through the Sensitive Peacemaking of Abigail

THE UNWRAPPING OF EMPATHETIC INTERACTIONS

When things are down and we are discouraged, we dearly want someone to feel our pain. We want others to have the empathy we need for healing and the encouragement to go forward. Unfortunately, empathy is a long lost trait and few of us know how to express it or receive it. Yet, we want it when things go sour in our life. Why have we not been taught empathy in school or in the home? For those who have been taught empathy, more power to them to live a life in which compassion and caring is shared with those in need.

Empathy comes from a caring heart, and a personal desire to share in the experiences of others. It is the perception and awareness that we desire to impact others emotionally at a time of need in their life. It is sensitivity for the feelings other people experience as a result of their encounter and interaction with us, in the world in which they live. It involves our taking action to get on the same wave length and move with and towards each other with compassion and thoughtfulness. It is the ability to create a sense of connectedness at a heart level with others.

It is vitally important to understand the feelings of others. People behave the way they do partly because they have certain feelings that provoke them to act in a certain way. Developing a sense of empathy can help us understand other people and, thus, get along better with them. Empathy serves as the backbone of emotional intelligence. It is important to note that we should not always be compelled to agree with others or support their feelings. It does not mean that one's feelings should excuse certain misbehaviors. On the other hand, feelings are part of the human condition, and we all have them. It is our understanding of our own feelings and the feelings of others that place us in a better position to master our interactions with others. Mastering our feelings involves taking responsibility for how we feel act and, and then, going about to change our feelings when appropriate.

Our interpersonal effectiveness is amplified as we exhibit an attitude of gratitude and express our appreciation to others through behavioral acts. Having an attitude of gratitude is a major component of empathy or interpersonal compassion. Gratitude is related to the management of our internal states, our inner thoughts and feelings. It is our internal perspective on things, with an emphasis of the world as a positive place and everything represents a gift. Attitudes of gratitude yield behavioral patterns of appreciation, both verbally and behaviorally. Remember, the attitude of gratitude and the skill of expressing empathetic sensitivity takes a lifetime to learn. The sooner, the better.

Empathy is learned behavior and is related to sensitivity for the feelings, plight and experiences of others. For example, parents who become aware of another child who is ill or in some type of trouble, could model and encourage their children to express and show support for that child at a time of need. Empathy is learned as children share something of themselves with those less fortunate.

It could be as simple as baking cupcakes and taking them to the classroom or daycare of developmentally challenged children. It could be giving money from their piggy bank or clothes from their closet to a family who suddenly became destitute as the result of their home burning down. Examples of need abound if we look for them.

EMPATHETIC INTERACTIONS AMPLIFIED BY ABIGAIL

Abigail was married to a loser. Nabal was an alcoholic. He caused distress everywhere he went. While Nabal was a wealthy Carmelite sheep rancher with a huge amount of livestock, he was known to be stubborn, bigoted, irrational, dishonest and ill-mannered. He was a known bully. He was often described as being worthless, and he made it difficult for others to approach him.

On the other hand, Abigail was held in sharp contrast to her husband. She was intelligent, beautiful, wise, and abounded with empathy. She was an "in charge" lady. She ran the home with efficiency and grace. She had all the hired help she needed. She knew what was needed for any given occasion. Her personal relationships skills were strong. Abigail was a strong woman who was prepared to come behind her husband and play the peacemaker role.

Nabal and Abigail lived during the time just prior to David becoming king, 1000 BC. It was around the time of Samuel's death. Nabal and Abigail lived in the area south of Palestine in the Sinai Desert. As their life unfolds, Abigail's empathy and wisdom was challenged in a significant and confrontational act which resulted in a unifying action in the life of the nation. It is a story that continues to have a significant impact on us.

During this time in history, there was a generally agreed employment policy that prevailed among the field workers and ranchers. The sheep had to be protected and sheered. It was the custom at the end of the year to tip or to give a bonus to the shepherds who worked during the year to protect and care for the rancher's animals. As the sheering time came, at the end of the season, it was time to pay-up. It was the time for appreciation to be expressed to the workers by tipping them and celebrating with a feast.

Six hundred of David's men, who voluntarily served with David, lived in the wilderness of Paran, near Nabal's ranch. While they were encamped there, David's men never stole Nabal's sheep or cattle or harmed his shepherds. Indeed, Nabal's shepherds considered David's men to be a wall of protection to them, as they looked after Nabal's ranch.

David sent 10 trusted young and determined men to ask Nabal for a year end contribution or gift of whatever was at hand for their assistance to Nabal's ranch and shepherds.

Apaprently, David's men arrived and approached Nabal at the wrong time. He was probably celebrating his successful year and was drunk. In any case, Nabal replied, with a jeer, to David's 10 men, "Who is David?" Nabal took a hard line and told the men he had no obligation to them and sent them back to David.

The 10 men returned from the fields to David and told of Nabal's unapproachable attitude and refusal to give them any gift. David quickly became enraged and responded with great anger. How unfair! How unreasonable! In his anger, David immediately gathered 400 of his 600 men and proceeded with swords in hand to prepare a march to the place where Nabal was located. A showdown was forthcoming. David was ready to confront this dishonest man himself and destroy Nabal's men. Nabal, himself, was a marked man.

At about that same time the servants of Nabal, who had witnessed the earlier confrontation between Nabal and David's ten men, went to Abigail and told the story of her husband's refusal to give a contribution or gift to David. Abigail listened attentively and empathically. She did not defend her husband as might be expected. She did not reject or negate those that came to inform her of her husband's folly. She did not reject their message. She tried not to add her own dismay in support of their frustration and panic feelings. She listened objectively and with empathy for all parties. In her wisdom, she put a plan together in haste.

Abigail took action. She began a process of compassionate peacemaking. Her intent was to put cool water on the head of David and buy time to get to her husband, Nabal. Immediately she gathered her servants from her household and prepared a huge feast which included 200 loaves of bread, 5 roasted sheep, 2 bushels of roasted grain, 100 raisin cakes and 200 fig cakes. She placed the food on donkeys and catered the meal out to the fields where David's men located. She wanted to avoid trouble for all concerned and hoped to appease David.

On her way out to the field, she came upon David who had just arrived on the scene and was about to confront Nabal. Again, her empathy and sensitivity skills came forth as she began to appeal to David for restraint. She knew how David felt after being insulted by Nabal, her husband. She knew her husband's behavior patterns when under the influence of alcohol. She knew and predicted how the situation could soon get out of hand.

As Abigail privately spoke to David, she first acknowledged her blame for the irresponsibility of her husband and his shameful ways. Secondly, she pleaded with David to withhold any planned action. Her exemplary attitude and feelings of empathy for both men was evident as she pleaded with David. As part of her negotiations she expressed concern that David not do anything to mar his reputation and jeopardize his honor in becoming king. She was very aware of David's honorable life and dedication to the Lord. She recalled and expressed how the Lord had protected him from vengeance.

Not surprisingly, she got David's ear. David listened to her. He gave her message serious consideration. He paused to weigh his options. He then responded and accepted her pleading. The conflict was defused. She was the peacemaker for the moment. Mission accomplished! David thanked her for being bold and keeping him from vengeance. Forgiveness was a difficult act for Abigail and the others, no doubt (see Appendix D).

Shortly thereafter, David and his men all celebrated with the meal Abigail had prepared. Abigail's faithfulness to her husband and her mild, compassionate and empathetic character won the day. Two weeks after learning about his stupid behavior from Abigail, Nabal had a stroke or heart attack and died. No doubt, Abigail kept David from taking the law in his own hands and allowed God to deal with Nabal through a health trauma and eventually death.

As time moved on, history unfolded for Abigail as the wife of King David. Abigail's life ends in a series of events that elevates her standing in the nation and with David. *Dare to be a sensitive peacemaker like Abigail at times of a family or friendship crisis!*

FURTHER READING ON EMPATHETIC INTERACTIONS

I Samuel 25:3; 14-44
Mark 2:1-5
2 Corinthians 1:3-4; 11:29
Colossians 2:1-5
2 Timothy 1:3-4
Hebrews 13:3
Philippians 4:14

DISCUSSION QUESTIONS

Empathetic Interaction Discussion Questions

1. Have you ever been in a situation similar to the situation in which Abigail, Nabal, and David found themselves? Can you identify with any of these people? Briefly, tell your story about how you were like one of these characters at a point in time of your life.

2. How do you deal with or cope with an alcoholic (drug abuse addict) father, husband, or brother?

3. Based on the definition of empathy in the initial paragraphs, how have you learned to be empathetic?

4. What would you advise one of your friends who needs to be more empathetic in his or her relationship with their spouse? How can any person become more empathetic and caring for their spouse?

Abigail Discussion Questions

1. Does it appear that Abigail enabled her husband to be irresponsible and continue his drinking pattern? What is a wife to do when her husband is addicted and creates one problem after another?

2. As a woman, was Abigail too bold in her approach to David? Should Abigail have responded differently to David? What would you have done?

3. Since Abigail knew a great deal about David and his future kingship, how do her actions indicate her strengths?

4. Could Abigail have acted in a better manner to help save Nabal from himself?

EMPATHETIC INTERACTION DAILY EXERCISES

1. Identify someone you know that is in need of help or support. Consider what you can do to intervene and be of help to that person. In so doing, try to get into the feelings and plight of the individual. Be caring and empathetic.

2. Pay close attention to your feelings and thoughts this week. Make note of each time you have an empathetic thought or

response to someone. Follow up as it is appropriate for the occasion.

3. Think of someone who is a very empathetic person and consider them to be a model for you this week. Practice expressing empathy to another person all week.

EMPATHETIC INTERACTION ARROWHEADS

- Gratitude is the dearest price that we proud mortals pay.
- Ingratitude chums around with selfishness and pride.
- The door-mat takes a lot of dirt but keeps the parlor clean.
- Which palm do you offer Jesus—the palm of the hand or the palm branch?
- We are not the way we are because we feel the way we feel, but we feel the way we feel because we are the way we are.
- You will not stumble while on your knees.
- 'Tis the ear that keeps us on our feet.
- Some Christians don't have enough salt to make a tear.
- Even the "mighty rushing wind of Pentecost" cannot stir the lake which is frozen over.
- Modern religion doesn't have enough blood to create a blush.
- The only fever germs in the Living Water are those that make us burn for lost souls.
- Some Christians are "rivers of living water," others will not give out a drop no matter how you pump them.
- The whole world was to be taxed but the little Stranger in the manger paid the bill.
- A child's heart is plastic as dampened sand, but give the cement of the will time to set and it will turn to stone.
- When charity blows a trumpet the poor starve.
- They that are past feeling have no desire and no satisfaction.
- Better a pound of feathers to the weary than a pound of gold.
- The preacher that has calloused feet does not have a calloused heart.
- One can easily be thankful for a rough road if that road leads home.

My Empathetic Peacemaking Arrowhead _____

MY WEEKLY JOURNAL OF EMPATHETIC INTERACTIONS

The *empathetic interaction* lessons I learned this week were....

INTERPERSONAL
SENSITIVITY . . . .

Through the Charitable Thoughtfulness of Rebekah

THE UNWRAPPING OF INTERPERSONAL
SENSITIVITY

Every parent wants their children to develop into socially sensitive and responsible adults. Some parents succeed, while other parents don't. Fortunate is the parent that reaps the joy of having raised mature, dependable and responsible children who live socially connected lives and who are helpful to those less able and less endowed. Social responsibility is not easily taught. It does not come naturally. It must be learned from those who intentionally teach social responsibility by example, direct instruction and encouragement.

The ability to acquire sensitivity and responsibility is essential to emotional intelligence. It involves the undertaking of assigned chores, following through on commitments, taking responsibility or ownership for one's contribution to a problem and willingness to commit to the resolution of that problem. Social responsibility is the act of taking an action and fulfilling an opportunity to serve and assist others in their daily living struggles.

It is when we are able and prepared to give up our own preferences, commitments, and desires, and respond to the needs and preferences of others, that we exhibit the essence of social responsibility. Social responsibility involves giving up what we have and what we want, so that others can experience what they need and want. Thereby we take into account and enjoy the personal benefits of the greater good for all. Interestingly, research at the California Institute of Technology has found that those who care for others, regardless of gender and species, will survive longer, as much as 20% longer, and enjoy a higher quality of life.

Being intentionally mindful of others is the essence of social responsibility. It is the ability to take responsibility for one's action patterns in various day-to-day situations. We often cannot change other people, but we can change our response to them and how we feel about them. It has been said, "What we are is God's gift to us; what we become is our gift to God." The lifestyle of serving others is the pattern of becoming and living out a life of God's gift to the world in which we live.

INTERPERSONAL SENSITIVITY AMPLIFIED THROUGH REBEKAH

Rebekah's life in the home of her parents was fairly mundane. Her household chores included a daily trip to the town spring to fetch water for the day's needs of the family. Upon arrival at the spring, she usually had to wait her turn to fill her water pot. While waiting, time was spent talking to all the other women also waiting their turn. The walk home with a full pot of water was a trick. She did not want to spill the water or stumble and fall which would result in a pot of wasted water, a scarce commodity indeed.

Soon after drawing water from the spring, an obviously thirsty man with many loaded camels approached her and asked for a drink. Without much ado, she graciously shared some water from her pot with him, and then she proceeded to offer water for the camels. She drew many pots of water until the 10 camels had enough to drink.

This act of altruism or caring was beyond the typical daily experience at the spring. Rebekah must have been motivated by a sense of social responsibility for those in need and a learned sense of compassion. It was beyond her call of duty while out on a routine family responsibility. It is important to note that the traveler watched her carefully to see if she was the answer to his prayers for his mission on behalf of Abraham. Prior to his appearance in town, the man stopped at the edge of town and prayed very specifically for the wisdom and sensitivity to know and make contact with the exact woman of God's calling for Isaac, the son of Abraham.

While this all seemed so mundane and neighborly, it all occurred at a point in time in Rebekah's life when she was ready for a change. It took an act of social responsibility to bring about the change. For example, Rebekah demonstrates socially responsible living as she was caring and thoughtful enough to share water, not only with the thirsty traveler, but also his camels. She felt sympathetic towards the tired camels and offered to give them water as well. She simply became aware of a need and responded to it fully. That is the essence of socially responsible living.

Little did Rebekah know that the man whom she had helped was Eliezer, the chief servant of Abraham. Eliezer had been sent out by Abraham to find a wife for his son, Isaac. The pursuit was not to be based on beauty. Rebekah was a beautiful young girl but because of her thoughtful actions and kindness that went beyond the ordinary, she was the assumed answer to Eliezer's prayers for a wife for Abraham's son.

Rebekah proceeded to invite Eliezer to come to the home of her parents and stay the night. He realized they were relatives of Abraham and agreed to stay. As the evening events unfolded, Eliezer explained to Rebekah's parents the purpose of his mission and his preference of Rebekah to fulfill his mission. The plan was for her to return with him forthrightly and be presented to Abraham as the chosen bride for Isaac. No doubt, much discussion took place in a short time around the table spread with food. There was much reluctance expressed on the part of her parents to send Rebekah so quickly. However, in due time, she assertively speaks up; "I will go." It was an act of faith along with considerable excitement. She was willing to go with a stranger to a strange land to become the wife of an unknown man. No small decision. It was a big moment in their life as a family even though Rebekah was actually going to an unmet relative of the family.

Rebekah began packing to be ready to go before the break of dawn. Eliezer prepared the camels for the return trip. The evening was filled with excitement mixed with anxiety. Unsureness gripped the home that evening. Did anyone actually sleep that night? In the morning, her parents blessed her with a special blessing as she, Eliezer and the servants departed.

The 500-mile trek was long, arduous and filled with questions as issues went through her mind every day of the journey. As the camel caravan came close to her future home, she came into eye-view of her future husband, Isaac, who was out in the field meditating, praying and waiting. Isaac spotted the camels coming. Excitement whaled up within him. This was the moment for which he was waiting. Isaac ran up to the caravan, spotted Rebekah and immediately fell in love with her. Her beauty was eye-catching. It was a "God moment" for Isaac, perhaps for Rebekah also.

Isaac brought Rebekah into his mother's tent, and they became husband and wife. Isaac quickly learned to love her and appreciate her. Their relationship flourished and matured. Together they began a life faithful to God's call. It continued and ended well. Her socially responsible act at the community spring led to a happy change in her life, her family's life, and in the life of Isaac and his family. *Dare to be socially responsible like Rebekah at times of someone's personal need!*

FURTHER READING ON INTERPERSONAL SENSITIVITY

Genesis 24-27
Exodus 15:26; 18:13-26
I Chronicles 9:22-27
Ezekiel 33:1-9
John 10:11-14
Romans 1:14-17; 15:1
Philippians 1:26
I Timothy 5:3-8
I Peter 4:4-6

DISCUSSION QUESTIONS

Interpersonal Sensitivity Discussion Questions

1. What grade on a 10 point scale would you give yourself on social responsibility? Why?

2. What are a few examples where you acted and thereby demonstrated social responsibility? What was the affect on you? On the other persons involved?

3. How was social responsibility taught and modeled in your childhood home? Have you followed this pattern or created your own pattern over the years?

4. Are you aware of an immediate situation in which you now need to act in a socially responsible manner? What is it, and what might you do?

Rebekah Discussion Questions

1. What is the main story of Rebekah as it relates to acts of mercy and social welfare?

2. What are the main points that separate a person with inner beauty from one with outer beauty? What did Jesus say about this distinction?

3. How could Isaac come to love her immediately? What were your thoughts about "love at first sight" between Rebekah and Isaac?

4. Did you come to like Rebekah in this story? Why? Why not?

5. Would you have liked to have been Rebekah's parents? How would you have responded to the situation differently?

6. Is this a story of social welfare? How is it different? What is social welfare based on this story?

INTERPERSONAL SENSITIVITY DAILY EXERCISES

1. What acts of social responsibility did you engage in this past week? What acts could you undertake next week as you are more aware of its importance and impact on others?

2. Look for an opportunity to give a cup of cool water to someone this week who is not expecting it.

3. Develop your own definition of social responsibility.

INTERPERSONAL SENSITIVITY ARROWHEADS

- Too many have chosen myopia as their Utopia.
- Much knowledge and little wisdom is like dynamite in a child's hand.
- The boaster is like a shallow river with a big mouth.
- Some people are actually knocked over with a feather—one feather in their hat and they topple.
- If you must give dirty looks, aim them at the mirror.

- Keep yourself balanced and you will have less trouble balancing your books.
- Pictures must be taken in the light but developed in the night.
- Keep directly beneath the sun and you will have your shadow beneath your feet.
- "Other" makes up the greater part of Mother.
- The candle serves and makes no noise about it.
- One turn of a rubber heel erases many a good deed.
- One person doing all the work will cause a dozen men to shirk.
- You can't stop the echo when once the word has passed your lips.
- A heavy load is seldom the cause of a broken back.
- Much knowledge and little wisdom is like dynamite in a child's hand.
- He who first treads a path directs the steps of generations after him.
- If adults would imitate the children it would be safer for the children to imitate the adults.
- The windmill is moved by its surroundings; the electric fan moves its surroundings.
- The most beautiful deed becomes ugly when you crow about it.
- Service is a better safety-valve than boasting for an overabundance of spiritual power.
- The wise men of Jesus' day presented frankincense. The worldly wise of our day present rank nonsense.
- What the world needs is mercy LIVING, not mercy KILLING.

My Interpersonal Sensitivity Arrowhead _____

MY WEEKLY JOURNAL OF INTERPERSONAL SENSITIVITY

The *Interpersonal Sensitivity* lessons I learned this week were . . .

INTERPERSONAL BONDING . . . .

Through the Friendly Relationship of Jonathan and David

THE UNWRAPPING OF INTERPERSONAL BONDING

We thrive on close relationships. Without them, we become depressed and lonely. We all know what it is like to go to events alone or to have no one to reach out to in a time of need. Aloneness is an eerie feeling. Being left behind is a sorrowful state in life and a most lonely one. We all have a story to tell about our experience in being left behind. Wow! That would be a depressing story book!

Interpersonal bonding involves keeping regular contact with friends and making time to connect with the array of significant people important to us. It is keeping the interpersonal gap closed. It also relates to our efforts to personally develop other people and being a person of influence. It means building and maintaining common bonds, managing conflicts and being able to achieve goals through team work. It is basic loyalty and trust. Honesty with oneself and with others is the opposite of being interpersonally phony. It is an essential trait of leadership.

A basic component of friendship is giving to one another and receiving from one another. We all have a need and a desire to belong. Friendship means the inclusion of others in our life so that we can contribute to their need for belonging, and they can contribute to our need for belonging. It does not mean taking ownership or taking advantage of others. Friendship is based on very simple skills, such as initiating conversation, smiling, shaking hands, offering compliments and praise, asking questions and responding to questions and comments put forth by others.

We all know the words of helpfulness, cooperation, consideration, caring and being responsible for others. These are very difficult words to put into action and make them a behavioral habit. As we engage in such behavior, we contribute to better relationships and to a better social environment.

Effective interpersonal relationships depend on our having learned "common courtesy" towards others. Common courtesy involves very simple behavior patterns which have profound effects upon others. For example, it includes saying "please," not interrupting others while they are speaking, sending thank you notes for gifts received, holding the door open for someone behind you, and greeting others freely and generously with a "hello."

At a higher level of consideration, common courtesy is based on several principles. These include, but are not limited to, the recognition that people are important, all people have value, and the way we behave towards others significantly impacts and influences their feelings, value and identity. Common courtesy reflects sensitivity to the feelings of others and an awareness of the importance of an honest, sensitive and caring relationship when dealing with others. This is the essence of bonding with others. (See Appendix B)

INTERPERSONAL BONDING AMPLIFIED BY JONATHAN AND DAVID

The golden example of a faithful and unselfish interpersonal relationship is that of Jonathan and his close and fearless friend, David. We all know David for his face-to-face stand off with Goliath. On the stony hillside looking down across the rippling brook and the dead body of Goliath, the life of David was soon to take a major turn in notoriety. By killing Goliath, David quickly became a hero. He was beginning his climb to become the nation's leader, even though he didn't know it.

It was soon after the death of Goliath that Jonathan and David struck-up their friendship. The bond that formed between these two men happened at a very important time in David's life and in the life of Israel. At the time, Saul was trying to control David and put limitations on him. In contrast, Jonathan was perceptive and noticed great potential and attributes in David. Over and over, David became strengthen by his new friend, Jonathan. Accordingly, he was able to meet many trials and overcome his oppressors. Over time, the two men not only struck a friendship but David became indebted to Jonathan. It was Jonathan who ultimately paved the way for David to become the greatest king of the people of Israel.

David's journey to the position of King was not without its ups and downs. People would sing his praises. Soon thereafter, those same people would be mobilized by King Saul to hunt him down and try to kill him. David was successful in learning how to hide. The assignments given David by King Saul were purposefully difficult. People expected and demanded much of David. Failure loomed in each assignment. Over the years, as David faced his trials, tribulation and opposition, he turned to Jonathan, his friend. It was Jonathan who guided him and supported him all the way in his long journey to become the King of Israel.

Who was Jonathan? Jonathan was the Prince of Israel. His father was King Saul, the ruling king at the time. As a result of his family standing, he himself was a rightful heir to the throne. However, Jonathan realized that David had greater potential than either he or his brother. Thus David was in a much better position to serve as king. Jonathan consistently demonstrated in his relationship with David the essence of friendship. For example, he saw value in David and advanced David because of his value even above himself. He didn't put himself down. He did not denigrate himself. Jonathan merely advanced the value, potential and the abilities of his friend above himself. Jonathan did not think in terms of his seniority or his rights, but rather who was the best person for the job. For Jonathan, the throne belonged to David free and clear. He served his friend accordingly.

The friendship between these two men involved a mutual investing of time and energy in each other. It was based on promoting the other over oneself. Jonathan took great pride and great reward in helping his friend succeed to the throne. Jonathan was truly a friend, but more importantly he was a king-maker.

Jonathan also took great encouragement and personal satisfaction in knowing that his friendship with David was an act of service to his God and to the future of the nation of Israel. Jonathan had an inside track. He personally knew the looming destruction of Israel because of the antics and the divisive personality of his father, King Saul. Jonathan did not want destruction to be the future of Israel. He saw David as being a unifier and one who could bring Israel back to its place of honor in the world's economic, political and religious systems. Jonathan always worked from behind the scenes through friendship. He was a committed friend, a sacrificial friend and unselfish friend of David. Jonathan chose not to compete with David for the cheers of the crowd or the blessings from heaven. He facilitated David's success and acceptance throughout Israel. Ultimately he proved to be the best friend of Israel as well as of David.

In summary, an interpersonal relationship is about empowerment, about strengthening and about advancing others over oneself. An interpersonal relationship is about picking-up others when they fall and helping them run the race faster, better and more efficiently. It is about teaching others how to become more effective and to advance the vision and the mission to which they are committed. Because of friendship, the race is run better than it would have otherwise. You can't be a true friend to another person unless you see their positive potential. You can't be effective unless you are faithful. You can't be the king-maker unless you are willing to sacrifice yourself and your own goals and visions for the good of someone else and for the good of a greater cause (See Appendix D).

Every great leader needs a Jonathan. Warm, committed, honest and trustworthy personal relationships do not come easily. Committed interpersonal relationships under-gird and strengthen every leader. Leaders with great potential may fail or become thwarted in their pursuit of worthy goals because they lack a "Jonathan" in their life. Leaders are empowered and encouraged through their interpersonal relationships with a "Jonathan" in their life, and when leaders grow weary and become discouraged, it is that person who steps up to the plate and helps rebuild and refocus. When victory is experienced, it is the "Jonathan" that steps back and admires the kingly one, the identified leader. *Dare to have a bond with a person like Jonathan for mutual support and encouragement!*

FURTHER READING ON INTERPERSONAL BONDING

I Samuel 11-19, 31
Psalms 119:74
Hosea 11:1-11
Matthew 2:15; 7:12
Mark 3:31-35; 12:28-34; 11:25
John 15:12-17; 19:26-27
Ephesians 2:1-10; 6:9
Colossians 2:1-2

DISCUSSION QUESTIONS

Interpersonal Bonding Discussion Questions

1. What are the qualities you possess that makes you a great friend to someone?

2. What interpersonal trait would you like to develop to better bond with someone in your life?

3. Give some examples of people with whom you are acquainted who demonstrate the qualities in a truly bonded interpersonal relationship?

4. Do you think there is a difference between interpersonal relationships in Jonathan's day as compared to the relationships we form in today's world? If so what is it?

5. Complete the questionnaires in Appendix A, B, and D.

Jonathan and David Discussion Questions

1. Share any examples in your life when you played the role of a "king-maker" or a great friend.

2. Can you think of any other Biblical or non-Biblical friendship that represents a good example of a healthy interpersonal relationship? Why?

3. Do you have a need for a Jonathan in your life? Do you want such a person? How would you go about acquiring such a relationship?

4. In what way can you be a Jonathan in the life of someone who is in need deserves such a relationship?

5. Discuss the following statement: *"God is compassionate, not because He chooses to be, but because He is*

compassion." Now apply it to yourself and to the relationship of Jonathan and David.

INTERPERSONAL BONDING DAILY EXERCISES

1. Go out of your way this week to connect with a new friend or with an old friend that you have neglected for a long time.

2. Make a list of 5-10 people you value and desire to keep in your inner circle of friendships. Think how you are going to foster these relationships over the next month or two.

3. Think about all the people you know. Who is most like Jonathan? How do the two of you most impact each other? Who do you know that is least like Jonathan? Could your relationship with that relationship be improved?

INTERPERSONAL BONDING ARROWHEADS

*   Our love is permanent only when we love the soul.
*   Truth and humility go hand in hand from the scene of an argument.
*   Walk backwards from the extravagant flatterer or he'll stab you in the back.
*   The backbiter is like a cat that will lie down and purr after he has eaten the canary.
*   If talk is cheap, then why do we pay so dearly?
*   Only the gossiper would be willing to be a "mouse in a corner," to hear things he shouldn't.
*   Ten thousand men can't hold one tongue but one tongue can hold ten thousand men.
*   'Tis a cheap friend that has a high price.
*   If it is not forgotten, it is not forgiven.
*   Do not measure the distance to a friend's house by a stone's throw.
*   The less thunder, the gentler the rainfall.

- Don't let the cold-shoulder sideswipe you into the soft-shoulder.
- Use your temper and you will not lose it.
- If you are always giving others a piece of your mind take heed lest you part with the last piece.
- I wish false tongues were as easily removed as false teeth.
- Pencil lead slays more than bullet lead.
- The gossiper, like the silkworm, spins his coffin with his mouth.
- The Great Physician also takes our temperature beneath the tongue.
- The tongue is the oldest spinning wheel and has spun a lot of yarn.
- The thankful soul always has something to share with others.
- Never take advice from the man who never takes advice himself.
- Meddlers are poor menders.
- Words are only the boxcars of a train of thought; how often they ramble empty.
- Kindness to others, like sunshine on a garden, brings out a rose where you think only thorns could grow.
- Gratitude is the dearest price that we proud mortals pay.
- God's children and the devil's children cannot play in the same back yard.

My Interpersonal Bonding Arrowhead _____

MY WEEKLY JOURNAL OF
INTERPERSONAL BONDING

The *interpersonal* bonding lessons I learned this week were....

PART III

THE SITUATIONAL ADAPTABILITY TRAITS OF EMOTIONAL INTELLIGENCE

Emotionally intelligent people come to know that life is not routine. For most, every day is different with changing schedules and new events that bring forth surprises of some kind. Decisions are then required as we negotiate these ever changing life events. Our overall success in coping with the changing environmental and situational demands on us is determined by our ability to effectively assess and adaptively respond to all events and circumstances that come our way. Often, we are required to respond to some situation with little or no warning or preparation.

To function effectively in today's world, we need to have emotional intelligence based on the skills of adaptable living. The primary traits of *situational adaptability* are comprised of Reality Awareness, Flexibility, and Problem Solving. All three are essential skills we need to develop so we can handle life's daily changes as they come to us, ready or not. As we are adaptable we can process the unknown and unexpected events of daily living and intentionally take positive action to shape our future.

Adaptability is not a sign of being spineless, but rather a sign of being personally strong, resilient and robust. Essentially, adaptability is related to our set of skills needed to assess a situation for what it is and forthrightly deal with it so that a purpose is fulfilled and a goal achieved. From this, good should emerge for the benefit of all concerned parties.

REALITY
AWARENESS . . . .

Through the Collective Wisdom of the Men of Issachar

THE UNWRAPPING OF REALITY AWARENESS

Ever confuse something that was unreal for something you thought was real? An illusion or a delusion would be examples. Reality assessment is the ability to evaluate the parallel or correspondence between what it is we experience with what actually exists in reality. It is comparing and lining up our subjective experiences with the objective situation we are facing.

Individuals are often described as being realistic, well grounded and perceptive if they speak factually and rationally about what is going on around about them. Reality testing is the act of separating the emotional overlay in a given situation from the rational or logical components. For example, everything we purchase, such as car, has factual and logical features to persuade us to buy or not buy it. However, a car also has a multitude of emotional and illogical factors associated with it on which we either buy the car or decide not to buy it. Our job is to ferret out the two factors and make a wise decision which balances the logical and emotional factors involved.

Reality awareness, or the assessment of reality, can best be understood by visualizing a *rational mind* based on facts, figures and objectivity. Then imagine an *emotional mind* based on feeling, subjectivity and the level of emotional arousal provoked by any given situation. Finally, imagine the blending or the overlapping of the rational and the emotional mind to become the *wise mind*. The wise mind balances the rationality and emotions when perceiving or analyzing a situation and taking a specific action. That is, wisdom recognizes underlying emotions within a given situation, but controls the emotional components from wanton decision-making. Wisdom gives weight to the rationality of facts, figures, and the various consequences associated with any alternative course of actions.

Testing our awareness of reality is a skill necessary to live life in an emotionally intelligent manner. It is a learned skill. We learn it from childhood as parents help us decide if a particular item we desire is a wise choice and worth the money paid for it. The learning process continues into adulthood as we buy bigger items, invest greater sums of money and assume greater risks. Wise decisions come about by blending our rational and emotional minds into a wise minded action or outcome.

REALITY AWARENESS
AMPLIFIED BY ISSACHAR

After seven years of fighting, the war finally ended with David being successful over the house of Saul. Upon the emotional death of Saul and by God's command, David traveled to Hebron to be anointed as their next king by the men representing the leadership of all 12 tribes of Israel. In addition, thousands of armed military troops from all 12 tribes soon gathered in support for David. They were all anxious to see David become King David and assume the responsibilities of the next King of Israel.

It was to this massive gathering and celebration at Hebron that 200 leaders of the tribe of Issachar came to show their support of David. The region of Issachar consisted of 16 cities and their associated villages. The boundaries fell between Mt. Gilboa and the hills of lower Galilee. It was located in the central region of Israel, just north and east of Jerusalem. Issachar was one of the 12 administrative districts eventually set up by Solomon. It was known as a workingman's territory.

Issachar himself was the ninth son of Jacob and was the fifth child to Jacob and Leah. His name means "man and wages," suggesting a man who was a hired worker. By the time of David, the tribe of Issachar had gained worldwide reputation for common sense and wisdom. The men of Issachar came to be noted for their wisdom and knowledge of the culture, as well as the political and social condition of Israel at that time. For example, in the Talmudic statement there was reference to the wisest members of the San Hedrin coming from Issachar.

The men of Issachar were able to evaluate the reality of what existed throughout Israel and the needs of the people of Israel at the time. They were able to evaluate the objective and the subjective elements of a situation or event about to happen. The men of Issachar were considered realistic and well grounded in what was going on around them throughout Israel. They were assertive men who spoke up and were able to articulate their thoughts, ideas, and their vision for the future of Jerusalem and Israel.

Why the distinction of the men of Issachar as "men of wisdom?" To be sure, the ability to test reality is the essence of wisdom, for which the men of Issachar were known. Perhaps this ability relates to their identity as educated and observant working class people. Perhaps it related to their ability to know what the grass roots people thought of Saul during his reign and the thoughts and ways of David as they knew him. Perhaps it was related to their location in the central sector of Israel where they were able to view the trade and travel trends of the people.

No doubt, because of the location of Issachar, personal relationships were formed with many people of all economic levels and from all the regions of Israel. Whatever it was, they distinguished themselves throughout Israel. They had achieved the honor of being known for being men of wisdom, men who knew their times, and men who knew who was in their best interest for the future of Israel, and they were able to articulate it in a reasonable and measured manner. *Dare to have the cultural awareness and wisdom like the men of Issachar at a time of national change!*

FURTHER READING ON REALITY AWARENESS

I Chronicles 12:1-39
Genesis 2:17
Psalms 51:10-13
Luke 17:20-21
I Peter 1:8-9
I John 1:1-4

DISCUSSION QUESTIONS

Reality Awareness Discussion Questions

1. Wisdom or thinking with a wise mind is the desired strategy in making decisions. Define wisdom. How is it different from common sense? How is it different from rational decision making? From emotional decision making? How do you come to think and make decisions with a wise mind?

2. Pretend you are going to buy a new car. What are the *rational factors* about the car and what are the *emotional factors* associated with the car you would like to buy? What are the *wisdom factors* that would lead you to actually buy it or not buy it?

3. Who do you know that makes wise decisions? How do they go about such decision making? Have you ever modeled

your life after them? How would you imitating someone who is a wise decision maker?

Issachar Discussion Questions

1. How would you learn to live a life like the men of Issachar? What are you doing now to move in the direction of becoming wise and assertive like them?

2. Who do you know that is a modern day Issachar? Why? How do you use that person as a model to live your life?

3. Have you ever been called upon to advise someone because they considered you a person of wisdom and that you know their circumstances under which they live? Share your experience and tell how it worked out.

REALITY AWARENESS DAILY EXERCISES

1. Pick a social or community problem and write out a brief statement of advice to the person in charge as to how you see the issue being resolved.

2. Describe the times in which you are living. Come up with 5-10 statements that describe the current lifestyle and times.

3. Work on becoming more assertive so you will be able to speak up when the opportunity presents itself about the conditions of the day, a current event problem, and your hope for the future.

REALITY AWARENESS ARROWHEADS

- If you cannot get your directions straight, get back to the place where you were born.
- If you are living, you do not need a birth certificate to prove it.
- The summer heat seems ten degrees hotter to the lazybones.

- The wing that dusts the hearth cannot pierce the sky.
- When the eavesdropper and the icicle begin to release what they have gathered, they plunge into the puddle below.
- The blunter the axe, the harder one must swing it.
- For every feather in the cap you need one in the wing.
- The shoe never fits some people's understanding.
- If you watch the clock one hour you will have lost one hour of your life.
- Sometimes it becomes necessary to shut one door before another will open.
- It is useless to prime a pump, which is stuck into an empty well.
- Measuring ourselves by the golden rule invariably turns it into a spanking stick.
- The goose with the uncanny ability to lay golden eggs should have more sense than to set on them.
- The brighter the background, the darker the shadow.
- How similar are dusk and dawn, and yet how vastly different!
- Whisper a lie and they'll believe every word; shout out a truth and they'll say, "It's absurd."
- On the see-saw of public opinion you will be up in the air one moment and down in a heap of dust the next.
- Secrets and men cannot bear to be popular.
- The pulse is a wristwatch which will eventually remind us of the late hour.
- The silver lining marks the size of the cloud, shows us the way around it, and gives us a sample of the other side.
- Our wisdom teeth come in last and go out first—perhaps because they find so little to feed upon.

My Reality Awareness Arrowhead _____

MY WEEKLY JOURNAL OF REALITY AWARENESS

The *reality awareness* lessons I learned this week were....

FLEXIBLE DECISION MAKING . . . .

Through the High Risk Journeys of Sarah

THE UNWRAPPING OF FLEXIBLE DECISION MAKING

How far do you bend to make something workable or successful? Flexibility is the ability to adjust behavior patterns, plans, emotions and thoughts to the demands of every changing situations and conditions in daily life. It is a mind-set of openness to new ideas, experiences and opportunities, and then taking advantage of them. It is the ability to tolerate situations that are unstructured and ambiguous. It is being able to change a strategy or plan when undertaking a task in the pursuit of a goal.

Being able to adapt to a change in circumstances and unexpected demands is vital to positive living. It is one of the key factors of adaptability within the spectrum of emotional intelligence. Positive and effective living requires us to be open to any and all unexpected changes in our plans, schedules and projects.

While none of us like being the one to change our schedule, our position on a topic or a decision, it may be necessary to do so for a win-win outcome to occur. Flexibility allows for new ideas to be expressed and digested rather than withheld or squashed. Flexibility allows for accommodation or compromise to occur so a win-win situation can result. Furthermore, flexibility allows a person to get unstuck so progress and forward movement are both facilitated and enhanced.

FLEXIBLE DECISION MAKING AMPLIFIED THROUGH SARAH

The life of Sarah, the wife of Abraham, was not one of routine, consistency, or predictability. It was not stable, to be sure. To live with Abraham, a man who lived on the raw edge of faith required the ability to be flexible. Life was a sequence of continuous God-directed adjustments for both Abraham and his wife, Sarah. As soon as she felt settled, it was time to move again, it seemed (Genesis 11, 12, 17, 18, 20, 21).

There were no dull moments in Sarah's life or home. She was an unusual woman. The events in her life that required her utmost flexibility and social adjustment were handled with grace and poise. It came about naturally for her, or God just gave her an extra amount of patience and tolerance for the challenges he put before her and Abraham.

First, when Sarah was 65 years of age, her world turned upside down. This was a time when most people were established and less likely to be flexible. It was a time when older adults had less tolerance for change, let alone a life of constant change. One day Abraham confided in her that God had spoken to him and asked him to leave Haran, his own country, and start traveling. He only knew he was to go to a land that God would later show him. Sarah was probably shocked. After all, she had already moved from Ur to Haran. However, when God spoke, Sarah listened and obeyed. The decision making process may not have been that easy, however.

After some time of packing and preparation, they were ready to leave home. God had told Abraham that if he obeyed, God would make him a great nation. Since Canaan was inland 600 miles from their home, Abraham and Sarah had plenty of time to do some thinking about God's promise. When they finally arrived in Canaan, God revealed another promise to Abraham, telling him that the land of the Canaanites would be given to his descendants. At this time, Abraham and Sarah had no children, as Sarah was barren.

It wasn't long before a famine broke out. It was time to move on again. Abraham was now told by God to head to Egypt, another 300 miles into the desert, further from home. As they arrived in Egypt, another traumatic time required Sarah's utmost strength and a willingness to be flexible. Since, Sarah was the daughter of Abraham's father, she was Abraham's half-sister, besides being his wife. If Pharaoh wanted her, they had agreed that Abraham would present Sarah as his "sister." Then he would be treated well and his life spared. They soon learned that Pharaoh wanted Sarah for his harem, as she was very beautiful. So, Abraham gave their agreed statement, and soon Sarah went to live in Pharaoh's harem. True to their thinking, Abraham was showered with many fine gifts. However, in God's divine plan to provide a way of escape and protection for Sarah,. God sent forth a series of plagues upon the house of Pharaoh. She was quickly returned to Abraham, and they were sent out of the country. God's plans had prevailed!

Sarah's flexibility was once again demonstrated in her desire of producing a son for Abraham, so God's promise could be fulfilled. Sarah concluded that she was the obstacle to the promise that Abraham would have a son. She devised a plan for Hagar to be the instrument through which Abraham would have a son, a common custom in patriarchal times. In so doing, she demonstrated her flexibility and her willingness to forsake her own desire to bear a son for Abraham. She presented the plan to Abraham. Once agreed, Sarah proceeded to give her maid, Hagar, to her husband so a son would be born of Abraham as promised. As a result and in time,

Ishmael was born. Unfortunately, this plan was not God's plan. Her creativity and flexibility went too far in her desire to help.

There was another time when Sarah's willingness to be flexible was required. God told Abraham that he was changing his name from Abram to Abraham (Father of Nations). He also changed Sarah's name from Sarai to Sarah (Princess). God also told Abraham that He would bless Sarah and give him a son from her, whom they would call Isaac (Laughter). There was never a dull moment for Sarah.

At age 90, Sarah faced another turning point. Her willingness to be flexible was again tested in a major way. Abraham frequently entertained unannounced guests and desired to treat them well. She had to rise to the occasion. Without much forewarning, he would summon Sarah to make cakes for his guests. At one particular time, after serving the guests and returning to her tent, she heard from the special guests that she would give birth to a son for Abraham. While flabbergasted, she laughed silently, as she was old, and Abraham was even older than she. Then she heard the words, "Is anything too hard for God?" As promised, Isaac was born the next year!

Sarah was indeed called to be flexible in raising her son! Hagar and Ishmael's behavior towards her and Isaac finally caused dismay and concern. Finally, Sarah's flexibility came to a halt, and she told Abraham to have them leave. Flexibility only goes so far . . . a line had to be drawn in the sand. It turned out to be a good decision, but not an easy one.

Years later, Sarah's need to be flexible was once again seen when she had to decide to allow Abraham to go to the mountains in the land of Moriah to sacrifice their son as an offering to God. This call on her was the ultimate flexible act of personal faith and marital commitment. Again, God provided a way of escape and victory. It was a stray ram that God provided for the sacrifice. Faith and commitment always win with God when we are flexible in following the light he shines along the path he lays before us.

As the historical story of Abraham and Sarah's life unfolds, we stand amazed. Abraham followed God for the rest of his life. Sarah followed too. They lived a nomadic lifestyle. Her flexibility skills were repeatedly called upon as her husband's dreams and visions took another turn in his pursuit of God's purposeful plan. Sarah shared the dangers and heartaches that Abraham faced. Abraham never really knew where he was going other than he was to be searching for "a city, which had foundations, whose builder, and maker was God." He followed God in faith. Sarah followed Abraham in faith as well. Faith was their shared commitment. It was the glue that held them together during the tough times of their travels.

In summary, their mutual flexibility allowed Abraham and Sarah to be mission focused and survive many difficult life events. Over time, they remained steadfast, yet flexible, and they . . .

- kept looking forward even when the circumstances of life changed.
- accepted the circumstances of life as they came and went.
- trusted in the Lord to protect them as the ultimate support person in their life.
- maintained a hope for the future.
- honored the Lord by following the path he laid out for them.
- allowed God to determine the right time to make their next move.

The rhetorical question remains . . . . Did God prepare her for this type of lifestyle during her childhood and early adult years? Did God give her special grace and ability to adjust to situations as they unfolded over the127 years of her life? *Dare to be flexible and risk—taking like Sarah at times of God ordained unknown risks!*

FURTHER READING ON FLEXIBILE DECISION MAKING

Genesis 11-12; 15-18; 21-22
Ecclesiastes 3:11
2 Timothy 3:16-17
Lamentations 3:22-24

DISCUSSION QUESTIONS

Flexible Decision Making Discussion Questions

1. How do you rate yourself on flexibility in everyday living? Are you above a 5 or below a 5 on a 10 point scale?

2. What do you suggest you can do to become more flexible and get along better with others?

3. Did you come from a family that was flexible and taught you to be flexible in family life and in your relationships? How was flexibility played out in your childhood home? Was your childhood home known for its inflexibility or flexibility? What about your spouse or friends?

4. What is good about being flexible? When is some degree of inflexibility a good thing? When might it be best not to be flexible?

Sarah Discussion Questions

1. Which of Sarah's experiences taught you a meaningful lesson in flexibility for the good of your marriage? What about your general relationships?

2. Could you be a "Sarah" in your marriage today?

3. Discuss the marriage relationship of Abraham and Sarah. If they were living today and were part of your church or neighborhood, how would you relate to them?

4. What advice would you have given Sarah or Abraham about their marriage at their going away party as they were ready to leave Haran?

5. Have you ever felt that God wanted you to be a Sarah or Abraham or have a similar marriage? If you had a similar experience to Sarah, what was it like and how did you cope with it for God's glory?

6. What if Sarah had not been flexible? What if Abraham had not honored God's call on his life? Any thoughts on the likely outcome for Sarah and for Abraham?

FLEXIBLE DECISION MAKING DAILY EXERCISES

1. Consider a journey that God wanted you to take, but you chose not to go? Discuss why you did not go and what affect it had on you for not going. Any regrets?

2. Consider when you did in fact undertake a journey that God called you to take. What affect did that have on you? Any lessons learned?

3. Write down on a piece of paper what you plan to do this week to increase your flexibility skills. Put the paper on your refrigerator. Review it daily.

4. Catch yourself being flexible this week. Give yourself a point for each time you became aware of being flexible. If you scored 12 or more such occasions this week, treat yourself to something you like. This game is called, *"Catch Yourself Being Flexible."* Keep doing it for the next three weeks while you are establishing a new habit of flexibility.

FLEXIBLE DECISION MAKING ARROWHEADS

- No question is unanswered if we need the answer.
- Be not like unto a brook going around every obstacle by the line of least resistance.
- If you are cornered, turn the corner inside out and go around it.
- Religion is like an apron which can be worn either to take dirt or cover it.
- This generation plays everything but safe.
- He who at the fork tries to take both roads will soon find his legs too short.
- Moving objects never fail to catch the eye.
- A camel will go through a needle's eye if you grind him up fine enough.
- If obstacles get in your way, do as the wind—whistle and go around them.
- You may stretch a point but it will give you a weak line.
- The closest we can come to getting everything we want is to want everything we get.
- There are but two ways to conquer a shadow—remove the object or turn out the light.
- Save a step and break a leg.

My Flexible Decision Making Arrowhead _____

MY WEEKLY JOURNAL OF FLEXIBLE DECISION MAKING

The *flexible decision* making lessons I learned this week were....

PROBLEM SOLVING . . . .
Through the Assertive Leadership of Nehemiah

THE UNWRAPPING OF PROBLEM SOLVING

Problem solving is not where most of us specialize. To the contrary, we all have a long history of making problems for our parents, teachers, coaches and scout leaders, to name a few. If asked to tell a story of some of the problems we created, we could probably do so without difficulty and with much enjoyment. On the other hand, we may find it much more difficult to tell a raft of stories of the problems we solved.

Unfortunately, problem solving is not a skill we were formally taught in school or in the home. How does one teach problem solving? Who is qualified to teach it to us? Where could we go to a class for such a purpose? For the next 10 minutes, I invite you to enroll in a course on "Nehemiah's School of Problem Solving."

Problem solving is the ability to perceive a problem, define the nature of a problem, consider optional solutions, and address it constructively. This is a lifelong learning challenge for all of us. Generating optimal choices, selecting the most reasonable course of action, and implementing the most potentially effective solution is the essence of the problem solving process. Problem solving involves the unique combination of decisive thought and strategic action. It involves an intentional and sequential series of steps to be taken towards the goal of resolving the identified problem. There are times we can only reduce the impact of the problem and its associated losses, but not completely solve the problem. We have to do the best we can in that situation.

Problem solving skills are critical to a life based on emotional intelligence. It is one of the most "learnable" social skills beginning in childhood. Children generally learn their problem solving skills without even being aware of it. It is a natural learning process based on our personal observations. We call this observational learning. Children then use this primary problem solving strategy throughout their life, often unwittingly. They learn to deal with people, events and situations directly by observing someone good at it. Some of us become good problem solvers. Others never quite learn the process and live a life marked with unresolved problems and hurt, often being a victim of those with whom they associate, who are also poorly prepared problem solvers.

The goal for children, and for adults also, is to acquire the ability to read situations, understand the social context that influences the way things are operating, and be able to choose behavioral strategies most likely to lead to success. Some problems are solved and other problems are avoided. Life on a higher plane can be experienced as we acquire strong problem solving skills and perspective, and then work to solve the problem.

PROBLEM SOLVING AMPLIFIED
THROUGH NEHEMIAH

It was 440 B.C. The walls of Jerusalem were decaying and crumbling from years of neglect and the gates were burned. The broken walls with gaping holes were a welcome sign to the enemies from without. The broken and fallen walls were a perceived safety problem facing the returning exiles to Jesrulsem, but only Nehemiah, an exile in Persia, decided to address it. It was a situation that demanded a solution, but first, he needed to pray about his concerns.

Nehemiah proceeded to pray and then to design a plan to solve the problem. As a cup bearer to King Artaxerxes of Persia, Nehemiah knew that the king needed to be approached with a detailed plan with a purpose and cost accounting components. He knew kings were not approachable without a full and organized plan to solve a major problem that might also be in the best interest of the king himself.

Four months later, the king brought up Nehemiah's health, which led Nehemiah to reveal his concern and plan to rebuild the city of his fathers. His prayers were answered. King Artaxerxes was moved by Nehemiah's passionate proposal and plan. Once the king understood the seriousness of the problem, he allowed Nehemiah to go to Jerusalem. He supplied Nehemiah with his requested materials and the necessary letters of recommendation. Nehemiah went willingly and with haste to Jerusalem. He was on a passionate mission.

Upon his arrival, a quiet detailed assessment of the wall was undertaken. He viewed the wall from the inside and the outside. Extensive notes were taken and recorded. After assessing the walls and developing an even more detailed and strategic plan. Nehemiah challenged the leaders and told them of King Arlaxexes agreement with the plan. They all agreed to the plan, and the work began.

The priests, leaders, men and families banded together to undertake the project and work on a particular section of the wall or gate. Stones were brought up the hill from where they had fallen over the years of neglect. Due to plots against them by their enemies, Nehemiah set up an elaborate security system so the work could continue. All the people worked on their assigned sections and completed the project in a remarkable 52 days, to the glory of God himself.

Nehemiah was the man for the job. He was a successful man. He was a strong and determined man. He was intense. He had a Type A personality. Being a governor twice attests to his public image, management ability, and leadership skills. He was a man of prayer and who readily acknowledged that God had been good to him. He was able to believe with confidence that as the people committed themselves to the task and relied upon God, they would rise to the occasion, rebuild the wall, and successfully complete the project (Nehemiah 2:18-20). The completion of the project led to celebration and a rededication of the people to follow the ways of the Lord, serve Him and not neglect the Temple of God. Before returning to the palace at Shushan, Nehemiah approached the new governor and gave thorough instructions regarding the gates of Jerusalem for their security.

In contrast, without Nehemiah coming back to town and giving leadership to this project, the people could have been chronic victims of the passivity of their leaders. They could have remained inactive and left to live under fear. The walls would have continued to deteriorate and remain in ruin. Jerusalem would have become one of the weaker cities in the region. The people would have continued to live at risk from their many enemies and competing kings and armies that lived beyond the walls of Jerusalem.

In summary, Nehemiah was a problem solving man. He was not afraid of problems. He had a passion to solve the problem of Jerusalem's wall. He was able to analyze the problem, develop a plan to solve the problem, obtain the support of the king and obtain the materials. He then mobilized people to join him and organized them to solve the problem. He created various work teams, and led the people in their tasks to completion.

He did not allow his distance from Jerusalem to avoid solving the problem. *Dare to be a determined problem solving leader like Nehemiah at times of leadership neglect!*

FURTHER READING ON PROBLEM SOLVING

Nehemiah 1-7
Matthew 8:23-27
Jeremiah 33:10-11

Philippians 1:12; 4:14
James 1: 2-4, 12
2 Samuel 22:30

DISCUSSION QUESTIONS

Problem Solving Discussion Questions

1. What is the biggest problem you have undertaken in the past 20 years of your life?

2. What was the strategy you utilized to get the involvement of others to help you solve the problem?

3. Was God interested and involved in the problem and its solution? How do you know?

4. What is your current level of problem solving orientation and skill? What do you need to learn so you can become a better problem solver?

Nehemiah Discussion Questions

1. What is the unique skill of Nehemiah that you admire and would like to possess?

2. Who is a modern day Nehemiah that you admire? Why? Describe that person.

3. Have you ever worked for or been associated with a leader like Nehemiah on a project in the past few years? Tell the story in brief.

4. Had Nehemiah not been moved to solve the "wall" problem, what would have been the outcome of Jerusalem over the next generation? What did he prevent from happening? Any modern day applications to this outcome for Jerusalem?

PROBLEM SOLVING DAILY EXERCISES

1. Name a problem in your community. How would you go about addressing the problem and solving it? Who would you need permission from to proceed?

2. Select a small problem to solve in your home, church, work, or community and design a way to solve it. Try to undertake the problem and solve it.

3. Write a Letter to the Editor of your local newspaper and outline a problem in your community and tell what could be done to solve it. Try to sell your idea to the readership.

PROBLEM SOLVING ARROWHEADS

- Too many have chosen myopia as their Utopia.
- Mend your ways today and you will have no time nor need to worry about tomorrow.
- If you cannot get your directions straight, get back to the place where you were born.
- An open mouth will soon empty the wisest head.
- 'Tis better to come to a dead stop than to a stop dead.
- Sometimes it becomes necessary to shut one door before another will open.
- Incubator chicks know nothing about wings.
- No question is unanswerable if we need the answer.
- We must pay the price of a clouded sky if we want the refreshing showers.
- The richest chords require some black keys.
- A dictator is one who rules everyone but himself.
- He who sails his ship in the gutter is soon stranded.
- Much knowledge and little wisdom are like dynamite in a child's hand.

My Problem Solving Arrowhead _____

MY WEEKLY JOURNAL OF PROBLEM SOLVING

The *problem solving* lessons I learned this week were....

PART IV

THE STRESS MANAGEMENT
TRAITS OF EMOTIONAL
INTELLIGENCE

Stress is part of our everyday life. We soon learn that stress cannot be eliminated, but that it can be managed. Some people are good at managing day to day stress, but most of us need some help so that our personal stress does not become overwhelming and defeating. Critical to becoming emotionally intelligent is the judicious management of daily stress.

Stress can be acute or chronic. Most of the stressful situations we face are acute, short term and circumstantial. When circumstances change because of our actions or the interventions of others, our stress is resolved. Once our stress level is reduced, life goes on.

However, some of us live with chronic and unabating stress. We must learn to live with it and cope with it the best we can. It is this latter type of stress, if left unmanaged that debilitates us, breaks us down, and creates a series of secondary problems. Usually our health takes its toll. Our performance becomes erratic. Our relationships suffer. Our sleep is impaired, and our sense of peace is taken from us, to name a few associated affects.

Stress management is made up of Stress Tolerance and Impulse Control. It is often our impulsive reactions that lead us into more trouble and additional stress. Stress management is based on thinking through alternative courses of action available to us before responding to a stressor. When these two skills are in place and well developed, we can withstand the stress while we are planning the necessary actions steps to resolve the stressful situation or manage it better. The options can then be weighed and we can begin the best alternative course of action available. While stress is harmful and destructive if allowed to linger unaddressed, it is useful if it motivates us to take wise and appropriate action.

STRESS TOLERANCE . . . .
Through the Forthright Determination of Job

THE UNWRAPPING OF STRESS TOLERANCE

Stress tolerance allows us to experience freedom from overwhelming feelings of anxiety, uncertainty, and nervousness under difficult and compelling situations. Stress events are arousing and overwhelming situations and circumstances in our life which need to be eliminated or well managed. Stress is inevitable. The more our level of involvement and responsibility in life, the more stress we experience.

Tolerance for stress is one of the main lines of defence we have against stress overtaking and overwhelming us. Tolerance for stress gives us time to work through solutions and develop a specific strategy for any given stressful situation we are facing. It is a key factor for effective daily living.

We have all known and have experienced some humiliating experience such as falling off a teeter totter, not being selected to play on a school team, or being restricted from participating in some desired social activities. We all have been unfairly attacked by people we respect and who are important to us. All of us, at some time in our life, have experienced an unanticipated personal disaster, through no fault of our own. To be sure, bad things do happen to good people. Stress is subtle and sneaks up on us. It can be persistent and require us to be tolerant of it if we are going to overcome it.

While we usually cannot eliminate stressful situations from coming into our lives from many different sources, we can learn to tolerate the stress while we are working on a solution to resolve it for good. The goal is resolution, but sometime we have to settle for stress management or even stress tolerance.

STRESS TOLERANCE AMPLIFIED BY JOB

The pre-crisis lifestyle and pattern of experiences for Job was stress tolerant. Until his older years, he lived a life of godliness, prosperity, respect, and high achievement, as well as having a healthy family life. As Job was winding down his productive years, he lived in the Land of Uz, now known as Edom. There he built a large mansion so he could enjoy the coming and going of his children, grandchildren and the multitude of friends he had made over the years. The story sounds fairly common and consistent with what most of us want and work to achieve as we age.

Unfortunately, "problem free living" was not God's plan for Job, especially as he approached his older years. Like a sudden change of wind, Job was left bankrupt, homeless, childless, friendless, and seriously ill. For a period of time he even lost the strong support of his wife, his life partner. As a result of his many crises in a short amount of time, he developed a physical malady that plagued him and terrorized him from head to toe and from his skin to the very core of his body. The malady was never named, but we could think of many diseases with such a level of pain and impairment.

The disastrous and stressful part of Job's story commences with the wind storm that collapsed his son's home and brought about the death of his 10 children. At the same time, all his livestock and most of his servants were killed or taken from him. Helplessness was his lingering plight, but Job tore his clothes, shaved his head, fell to the ground, and worshipped God. Not long afterwards, sores erupted from his feet to his head so that he just sat on the heap of ashes in anguish and grief. His sores were so noticeable and repulsive that it was impossible for others to even recognize him or look at him. Job's wife was so stressed that she told him to curse God and die!

Job's disaster continued and exacerbated as three of his friends came to visit, but after days of silence, in an effort to explain all his disaster, they began a barrage of reasons and errors to account for it. They soon began a taunting, harassing and abusing barrage of criticisms, condemnations, accusations, insults and name calling. He experienced no help, little support, and little solace when he needed it most. The words and treatment of his friends must have rocked Job to his very core with anxiety, anger and depression. His stress was mounting. He appeared to experience something like a post trauma stress disorder.

However, drawing from his deeply embedded faith, God led Job to begin to turn the tables on his despair and pain. Job reaffirms his faith, and calls his friends to do the same. He stopped listening to and arguing with the deprecating words of his friends. He stopped looking and feeling dejected. Instead, he turned and looked skyward and talked to his God; the God he knew and communed with throughout his early and adult years. Again, for Job, God was there to speak with him, understand, support, and give him answers. Job did not turn on God and curse him, but rather let God be God.

His faith based "stress management plan" gave him tolerance for stress, allowing him to live above the awful circumstances. Job affirms his faith in God on a deeper level, and at God's prompting, prays for his friends. Job began to experience peace as he receives God's favor and his restoration. Job went on to recover, and God restored his fortunes, doubled his possessions, renewed his friendships, and blessed him and his wife with 10 additional children. Job was able to live a life of personal effectiveness and productivity until his death, years later. Further, Job reaffirmed himself, renewed his faith in God, and resisted the temptation to retaliate and seek revenge to those who had been disloyal. Instead of revenge, he disregarded the hurtful statements of his friends and wife and refocused on a strategic plan by which to rebuild his life to the glory of God.

Although his wife wavered earlier, she became strong in her support and hung in there with him to the end. She remained committed and faithful. She helped him start over, and together they achieved a new life, blessed by the very God he honored and relied upon in his darkest moments of despair.

Job's story concludes with a happy ending. He suffered the grief of incredible losses. He felt the unfairness of false accusations. He knew the urge of retaliation and reprisal. His pain and suffering were beyond the imagination of all of us. Yes, Job experienced stress at its worst, but emerged well through it. He came to value his suffering by keeping perspective of who he was and the ultimate purpose of his life. He discovered that self-knowledge and self-judgment is the prelude to greater fruitfulness. He was able to maintain a sense of priority. At one time, Job looked into the very face of death and into the very face of God, himself. Stress did not kill Job. Job killed stress.

He learned, for example, lessons in personal closeness. These lessons included closeness with God, closeness with his family and closeness with his social world. He also learned the power of forgiveness. (See Appendix D) He learned the lesson of starting over again. He learned the lesson of celebration. And best, he learned that ultimate peace comes from a deep relationship and reliance on God. Finally, he learned the faith-based lesson of stress tolerance. Though dead, he yet speaketh. *Dare to be determined and stress tolerant like Job at times of personal trauma and disaster!*

FURTHER READING ON STRESS TOLERANCE

Job 1-42
Exodus 23:9
Psalms 123:3-4
Matthew 26:37-46
Romans 14:1-8
2 Timothy 2:10

DISCUSSION QUESTIONS

Stress Tolerance Discussion Questions

1. Name some recent stressors in your life or in the life of your family. Why did they create stress for you? Did you handle them well? Why? Why not?

2. What are the primary stress management strategies you generally employ?

3. When you cannot avoid or change a stressor in your life, how do you tolerate it?

4. How do you pray for and expect God's help in tolerating or managing your stress?

Job Discussion Questions

1. In what way do you admire Job and the way he handled the most stressful time in his life?

2. Discuss some of the lessons Job learned through his encounter with God at a time of tragic stress? What lessons did you learn through your recent encounters with God at a time of tragic stress?

3. Discuss stress and its relationship to health. Has stress affected your health? Use job as an example of the stress-health syndrome.

4. Job struggled in his relationship with his friends and wife, but not with God. Why?

STRESS TOLERANCE DAILY EXERCISES

1. Write a brief story of your experience with a stressor and how you managed it and what you learned from it.

2. Discuss a stressful situation you are now facing and are trying to tolerate or manage better with someone.

3. Together with someone, draft an acronym of the word STRESS. Tell a story of stress tolerance in your anachronism.

4. How you can reduce the stress in someone else's life this week?

STRESS TOLERANCE ARROWHEADS

- One person can rest easier on a picket fence than another on a feather bed.
- Most of our fears are only scarecrows.
- We must pay the price of a clouded sky if we want the refreshing showers.
- Do not fear the shadows for they merely prove the existence and nearness of light.
- We cannot reach tomorrow, and in trying we lose today.
- There is but One who can adjust our sail, to make a motive power of the gale.
- Keep directly beneath the sun, and you will have your shadow beneath your feet.
- He who lives in the tomorrow has worry and fear as his comrades.

- He who kicks continuously soon loses his balance.
- People who have insomnia should try praying before they retire.
- One can always get a foothold when the road is rough.
- Less hurt—less worry.
- A wound will not heal if you keep digging in it.
- We stumble over pebbles not mountains.
- When you bury the hatchet, don't leave the handle sticking up for a marker.
- The brook would lose its song if you removed the rocks.
- Getting into hot water may merely diminish the fever that got us into it.
- He who lies down on the job will not have a very comfortable bed.
- If we were sufficiently worried about our past, we would not need to worry about our future.
- If you are swept off your feet it is time to get on your knees.
- He who goes around with a chip on his shoulder is likely to get the block knocked off instead of the chip. Remember Goliath.
- You may be packing for a long journey even though you only have a little "grip."
- The rain makes us sleepy, but we can't go to sleep if the faucet drips.

My Stress Tolerance Arrowhead _____

MY WEEKLY JOURNAL OF STRESS TOLERANCE

The *stress tolerance* lessons I learned this week were....

IMPULSE CONTROL . . . .

Through the Proactive Understanding of Manoah's Wife

THE UNWRAPPING OF IMPULSE CONTROL

Contrary to popular, but misleading belief, we can learn to control our impulses. How are you doing in this area of your life? This skill is one of the most important qualities of emotional intelligence. It is the ability to resist and/or delay our strong urges, drives and temptations. It is the ability to live life with an extra measure of patience, tolerance and moderation. The control of our strong impulses, wanton thoughts and undisciplined behavior is the primary objective for learning self-discipline and the pursuit of a defined goal.

Practicing self-discipline skills is foundational to becoming a mature adult and an emotionally intelligent person. The process of impulse control involves proactive thinking about our behavior and its consequences, selecting the proper choice of optional social behaviors, and utilizing self-reinforcement when engaging in positive thought patterns and the proper choices of activities. We know we have achieved impulse control when we are able to respond calmly, slowly and delay important decisions until adequate consideration has been undertaken. Impulse control generally contributes to a sense of self-discipline, accomplishment, self-mastery, and self-satisfaction.

Children as well as adults need the ability to control their impulses in a wide range of life situations. While some appear to have an inborn ability to control impulses, everyone can learn skills to gain better mastery over their impulses. Learning strategies for dealing with stressful situations in life, where we have to make choices about how to act, is the most difficult aspect of impulse control. Making careful choices and the right choices, as well as timely choices before acting, is what impulse control is all about.

IMPULSE CONTROL AMPLIFIED THROUGH MANOAH'S WIFE

The mother of Samson is simply referred to as Manoah's wife. She was not specifically named for some unknown reason. Her story might tell us why. She was known for having a stronger character than her husband, Manoah. For example, when an angel appeared to her, she exercised constructive impulse control and was known for her reverence, silence and obedience to the angel's voice. She was full of faith. While her faith remained unshaken, in contrast, her husband reacted in fear and pessimism. She was a wife who had a simple trusting confidence in God. She was a mother who was willing to sacrifice her own desires and impulses and concentrate on what was best for the family and others. She outdid Manoah on these matters. Does that give a hint why she was unnamed?

Manoah's wife set a spiritual tone in the home. She and her husband regularly offered up burnt sacrifices to God in grateful praise for his protection. Although she was barren, her husband encouraged her to patiently wait on the Lord to exercise the control of her impulses by her husband. He encouraged her to wait and act in God's timing. God honored her outward lifestyle of impulse control, her godly living, and her faith. One day, she was told by an angel's visit that although she was barren for so long, she would conceive and have a son. She was also told not to drink wine or any strong drink, and not to eat any unclean thing. She was also informed by the angel that her child would be dedicated to the sacred calling of a Nazarite, a calling that demanded the mother to be clean and of high self-control and self-discipline. As a mother with a purpose and calling, she then taught her son that no intoxicating drink should ever enter his lips and that no razor should ever touch his head. His long locks were to attest and speak of his sacred dedication to God.

There were two occasions in which the Angel of the Lord appeared to her. This suggests that she lived close to God and her lifestyle was pleasing to God. Her faith and her ability to exercise self control was seen when her son, Samson, chose to marry Timnath. Both she and Manoah objected and protested. They both tried to dissuade Samson from marrying outside the covenant people. Yet, he persisted. They eventually relented and exercised control over their feelings and went to the wedding, witnessing their son's marriage to the woman with whom they both had objections. They both held their tongue and objections. While Samson knew of their objections, they did not overreact and make a scene. No doubt they were so tempted. They let God direct the outcome of the unpopular marriage. Quickly, the marriage turned sour and soon came to an end.

In time, Samson became a very imminent Hebrew judge. His greatness no doubt was influenced by his mother's godly lifestyle and her early teaching in biblical character building. Self-control was a key temperament trait for any judge. Samson, most likely learned some self-control skills from the life skills training of his mother. Unfortunately, he learned his spiritual vitality the hard way, often disregarding the desires of his mother.

As history unfolded, he led with distinction and courage. Samson was later named as a hero of the faith. May we have the courage to live as the wife of Manoah and the mother of Samson. May we have the courage to live a life of self-discipline and self-control as was lived in this home. *Dare to be a proactive, understanding, and patient wife (husband) like Manoah's wife at times of spiritual and family events!*

FURTHER READING ON IMPULSE CONTROL

Judges 13, 14, & 16
Proverbs 16:23
Ecclesiastes 5:2
James 3:2
Revelation 21:10
2 Peter 2:19

DISCUSSION QUESTIONS

Impulse Control Discussion Questions

1. Why is it difficult to control your impulsive reaction when something you want is denied? What works for you when you must control your instinctive impulses?

2. Does the lack of impulse control constitute a sin or does it result in sin in our lives? Or, is it not a sinful act at all, but something else?

3. Consider your personal story of how you learned to control your impulses. Feel free to share your story with someone.

4. Who is your example or hero in the area of impulse control? Why?

5. The control of our emotions is a life time struggle. Do you need more training or help in controlling your emotions? Is there an area in your life where you have good control of your emotions? Is there an area of your life on which you are currently working to acquire more self-control? Can someone be of help to you?

Manoah's Wife Discussion Questions

1. If you were Manoah's wife, would you have undertaken a different course of action under the circumstances they were facing?

2. What do you admire in the personality and lifestyle of Manoah's wife? Why? Is she an example to you in some way?

3. What would you have done in dealing with the wedding situation she and Manoah faced? Could she have handled that wedding situation better? What advice would you have given her? Have you ever been in a similar situation?

4. Samson had difficulty accepting the lifestyle of his parents, especially that of his mother. Have you had a similar experience in the years of your youth?

IMPULSE CONTROL DAILY EXERCISES

1. Monitor yourself this week and catch yourself succeeding in the control of your impulses. Note how you are improving in moderating your response pattern.

2. During the week, plan an event or action, but carry it out over an extended time period as a way to learn impulse control.

3. Notice someone around you engaged in an impulsive act and try to slow them down in carrying out their intended action.

4. Think of three to five advantages for intentionally and deliberately taking a slow course of action in some activity or decision in which you are engaged.

5. Give yourself a compliment each time you notice you have exercised control over an impulsive act, urge, or thought.

6. Ask God to help you be aware of situations and decisions which require a good amount of impulse control.

IMPULSE CONTROL ARROWHEADS

- The hot-headed person is like unto a match—a bit of explosive on one end of a dry stick.
- When you worry about tomorrow you have concern for that which is not yours.
- Emotion is not so likely to run away if you hitch a good load to it.
- Pencil lead slays more than bullet lead.
- Work the brain ten hours to one of the tongue.
- It is too late to hold your tongue after it gets red hot.
- You can't stop the echo when once the word has passed your lips.
- Unbridled enthusiasm is as dangerous as a runaway horse.
- Every hobby horse should have a hitching-post.
- We know how to abbreviate most everything but trouble.
- "Strike while the iron is hot" may be a good rule but you better make the tongue an exception.
- He who speaks first and thinks later reflects on fool's talk.
- A "bit of love" is the only bit that will bridle the tongue.
- Anger, like the avalanche, blazes a trail which it never again uses.
- If a fool could hold his tongue he would find a place among the wise.
- Beware! Even a pussy-foot has claws.
- Tell all you know and you'll lose all you have.
- You who ask everyone to "wait a minute," why not demand it of your temper?
- One drop of water over the edge causes many more to overflow.

My Impulse Control Arrowhead _____

MY WEEKLY JOURNAL OF IMPULSE CONTROL

The *impulse control* lessons I learned this week were....

PART V

THE MOOD MANAGEMENT TRAITS OF EMOTIONAL INTELLIGENCE

Emotionally intelligent people are optimistic and happy. They have acquired the two moods that are the hardest to learn, develop and maintain. For most of us, we look outward and beyond ourselves and wait for others to do something that will give us cause to be optimistic or happy. We usually give little attention to the way optimism and happiness is developed. Some of us even think that we are entitled to those things that we think brings happiness. We then live a life dependent on someone to create a constant flow of events and circumstances that bring about our optimism and happiness. Entitlement thinking is part of this orientation, but it does not develop deep or true optimism or happiness. It does, however, create a thought process based on false hope.

Mood management consists of strengthening the two primary traits, Optimism and Happiness. The degree to which these two traits are present within us indicates our general feeling of daily contentment and our overall outlook on life. Those who maintain a balance of optimism and happiness are easy to be around. They are more likely to have effective interpersonal relationships, success in their undertakings, and enjoy life; however it flows from day to day. People are drawn to those who are optimistic and happy. They are viewed by others as highly functioning individuals. They are often sought out for friendship and leadership roles.

In times of tragedy, those that maintain a sense of optimism emerge as leaders and become a source of strength for others. Tragic life events can promote defeatism or hope. The term "tragic optimism" originated out of World War II and the experiences of those that survived life in the concentration camps. Tragic optimism is the belief that the tragedy will end some day and that survival is possible and will come, but the time is unknown. In brief, we can be optimistic in the face of tragedy.

Further, true happiness is not dependent on the good things that come our way. Rather, it deepens and grows out of a sense of contentment and optimism. Optimism and happiness go together. We might even call them the "kissin'cousins" of mood regulation and what we now recognize as major aspects of emotional intelligence.

OPTIMISTIC
THINKING . . . .
Through the Experienced Insight of Moses

THE UNWRAPPING OF OPTIMISTIC THINKING

Ever since childhood, most of us have been urged to look at the brighter side of life. Most mothers make it their mission to raise their children to be positive and upbeat. This task requires her to be undauntingly committed to the hope of an optimistic home and positive thinking children.

The ability to look at the brighter side of life and maintain a positive attitude, especially in the face of adversity, is the essence of optimism. Hope and expectation for a positive outcome are essential components of optimism. Optimistic people tend to select the most hopeful view of a situation and expect the best possible outcome of any given circumstance.

Essentially, optimism stimulates a sense of faith in oneself and others. How we think has a profound influence on how we feel and how we behave. If we think optimistically or positively about a situation that has occurred, we tend to feel better about it than if we think negatively or pessimistically. Likewise, if a student thinks of himself as being able to do better when he receives a low grade he will learn from the experience, and actually follow up by behaving in a manner that will yield a higher score on the next assignment.

Optimism creates collaboration and mobilizes people towards a common goal. Optimism replaces bigotry with understanding, openness, and hope. Indeed, there is the possibility of power-living in optimism. It is living one step beyond one's own safety zone. It is the willingness to act with reason while taking a risk or undertaking an action which is unpopular or unknown.

Further, when facing a tragedy, it is possible to think hopefully about the options and future outcome rather than thinking hopelessly about the likely outcome and the future. The term, "tragic optimism," was coined by the WWII survivor, Dr. Victor Frankel, who later became one of the world's foremost psychiatrists. Tragic optimism, thinking optimistically in the midst of a tragedy or crisis situation, made the difference for those interned in concentration camps in times of war. Those that considered their situation with optimism were the ones that had a better survival rate and outcome.

OPTIMISTIC THINKING AMPLIFIED BY MOSES

Moses knew the experience of optimism well. He is one of our prime historical teachers about optimism for today's world. It was the optimistic thinking of his mother who placed him in a basket in the Nile River to save him from Pharaoh's decree. No doubt Moses was profoundly affected when he later learned of the courageous optimism of his mother. As a young man, Moses killed an Egyptian while defending one of his own Hebrew people. For that, Pharaoh wanted to execute him and vigorously sought him. Moses ran to Midian, leaving the comforts of the palace and a life of ease behind him, and began a shepherd's life.

Many years later, Moses had an encounter with God as he stood before the burning bush. This was a turning point that helped Moses commit himself to an optimistic future defined by God. His natural pessimistic response changed to optimism as his faith rested in the Sovereign God. His deep faith in God spurred his optimistic thinking. At that point, the next 40 years of his life were determined. He systematically entered into a mature, faithful living relationship with God. His relationship with God was clearly revealed to others by his optimism and his positive encouragement to his followers. He was willing to take a risk for God.

Moses stood out from the crowd with his ruddy face, confident composure, and strong posture. As Moses stood among his people, his positive message of optimism was seen in sharp contrast to the depression, confusion, dismay, uncertainty, fear, frustration, and anger displayed by the people of Israel. Moses' optimism was also noted in sharp contrast to the cynicism, sarcasm and anger of King Pharaoh before whom Moses stood and pleaded for the release and freedom of his people (Exodus 32).

Again, Moses' optimism stood in sharp contrast to the helplessness that portrayed the two million complaining people who stood at the shores of the Red Sea with the ground rumbling beneath them as the King's army rapidly and fearlessly approached. It was Moses' faith in God and optimistic thinking at a time of impending tragedy that caused God to separate the sea and make a way for the Israelites' successful and historic escape (Exodus 14-15). Likewise, it was Moses' faith inspired optimism that prompted the people to take their first steps into the parted sea and witness God rescue them from their Egyptian bondage!

In summary, optimistic thinking is a learned and foreword way to design an action plan. It is looking tragedy in the face and responding with forward and hopeful thinking when all others only see hopelessness. Optimism is taking small chances. It is thinking that the best is yet to come. It is seeing the future to be brighter than the tragedies of the present or past. Most importantly, optimism grows stronger out of a rock-solid belief in God's presence, power, and protection while taking faith based steps into an unknown future. For Moses and all of us, optimism is a daily life-choice on the theme, "Is anything too difficult for God?" *Dare to be insightful and optimistic like Moses at times of choices and options!*

FURTHER READING ON OPTIMISTIC THINKING

Exodus 2, 14, 15, 32
Psalms 42:5; 73:12-28; 121:1
Proverbs 17:22
Jeremiah 29:10-11
Haggai 2:15
Romans 4:18-22
Philippians 1:3-6

DISCUSSION QUESTIONS

Optimistic Thinking Discussion Questions

1. What is the essence of optimistic thinking? How does it differ from faith?

2. Do you have a need for an optimist in your life? Do you want such a person in your life? Why? If so, how do you acquire such a relationship?

3. How can you become more optimistic? How can you be a reasonable optimist in the life of someone who is in need?

4. What does your optimism bring to the life of your family, church and work?

Moses Discussion Questions

1. What are the optimistic traits and actions you appreciate about Moses? Why?

2. Who is your modern day Moses? How does this person's life encourage you?

3. Do you think Moses acquired his optimism from his mother as a child or from his faith in God? Who has contributed to the development of your optimism, or the lack of it?

4. Tell how Moses stands out as a hero for you as someone to try to emulate.

OPTIMISTIC THINKING DAILY EXERCISES

1. Look in the local newspaper for a story in which optimism was portrayed. Tell the story to someone and underscore the element of optimism.

2. For the next week, catch someone being optimistic and commend them for it.

3. For the next week, catch someone being pessimistic. Challenge them to change their ways of thinking and talking to be more optimistic.

4. What is it about Moses that serves as an example for you to desire to become more optimistic in your thinking?

OPTIMISTIC THINKING ARROWHEADS

- The opti-MIST soon lets the sunshine through but the pessi-MIST never.
- The goose with the uncanny ability to lay golden eggs should have more sense than to set.
- Anticipated evils often obscure joys we dare not hope for.
- Reaching high keeps us on our toes.
- The smallest patch of blue will let the sun shine through.
- If you lack opportunity try importunity.
- There is no use in turning over a new leaf unless you turn out a new line.

- Much pure snow has fallen in the night.
- You can die without hope but you cannot live without it.
- We must pay the price of a clouded sky if we want the refreshing showers.
- The way of life is the only road which does not come to a dead end.
- The bottom will never drop out of your hope if it rests on the Rock of Ages.
- If you would hitch your wagon to a star, hitch it to the Morning Star.
- Seeing does not always believe, but believing is always seeing.
- You can go a long way with an empty purse if you are thankful.
- Learn from the hen that scratches her way from the barnyard to the garden.
- The place where we say to God, "Thy will be done" will spring into perennial bloom.
- The brook would lose its song if you removed the rocks.
- Mountain-climbing keeps us on our toes.
- You may wish upon a star but to get your wish you must follow it as did the wise men.

My Optimistic Thinking Arrowhead _____

MY WEEKLY JOURNAL OF OPTIMISTIC THINKING

The *optimism* lessons I learned this week were....

HAPPINESS
SPREADING . . . .
Through the Faithful Servanthood of Onesiphorus

THE UNWRAPPING OF HAPPINESS SPREADING

Historical belief holds that happiness is experienced when we feel satisfied and content with life, appreciate comfort from others and derive pleasure and enjoyment from our daily living experiences. It is considered a reactive emotion. We usually think of happiness as being a situational state of mind. We generally believe it depends upon circumstances in one's life at any given time. It naturally carries the implication of external influence. That is, one can be happy or unhappy depending on what other people do or say and the circumstances under which one lives at any given time.

Recent research indicates that happiness spreading is also a choice. For example, a happy smile produces increased brain activity in the frontal part of the brain, generally considered to be the area associated with good feelings. No wonder it was popular for children to sing, "Smile the clouds away, night will turn to day;

if you smile and smile and smile, you'll smile the clouds away." Indeed, we can procure happiness as we can learn to resist sadness and the negative moods related to stress.

Other research has found that pleasant moods, including happiness, can be triggered by pleasant scents much the same way that receiving a desired gift prompts a pleasant mood or reaction. The feeling of happiness and pleasantness appears to be directly related to a variety of environmental conditions and factors we create or that are imposed upon us.

However, long lasting happiness has been found to be associated with how we impact other people so they will experience a level of meaningfulness, satisfaction and enjoyment in their day to day living. It has been said, "Happiness is like jam: You can't spread it without getting some on yourself." Friends share joy together and they buffer stress for each other. This reduces the probability of having a health problem also. Research has found that women with 10 friends are happier than those with five friends, and they are more cheerful than those with no friends. However, the quality of the friendships always trumps the number of friends one has. The friendships that matter are those that create a sense of being cared for and supported by another. The more one has of such friends, the better. Also, we can have a major contributing influence on the level of happiness, satisfaction and quality of life of those with whom we associate and come in contact with each day.

We all know that life is not fair. Relationships and life experiences are far from perfect. Let that not stop us from doing the right thing, to bring pleasure and meaning to the doorsteps of our family, friends and acquaintances. Daily, we need to light our internal candle of compassion, thoughtfulness and friendship for others to experience happiness. Then, they will benefit and so will we.

HAPPINESS SPREADING AMPLIFIED BY ONESIPHORUS

Onesiphorus knew and lived the secret of happiness spreading. He was one of those saints who operated behind the scenes for the good of others. He was identified as a servant leader. His purpose in life was to encourage other believers. His focus was on facilitating personal strength and happiness through the process of encouragement. Onesiphorus was quick to offer hospitality to Paul whenever he came to town. It would appear that Paul and Onesiphorus spent long hours of conversation reflecting on Paul's recent ministry experiences, his influence on the church, and planning how he could minister even better. Paul was not one to engage in self-defeating talk such as blaming or whining which will squash anyone's happiness.

One can imagine that Paul and Onesiphorus talked late into the night. Onesiphorus was the student and Paul, the teacher. This is always the benefit of hospitality, being educated by the guests. Onesiphorus was likely the one to know more of Paul's experiences and ministry than most others.

Interestingly, it was not Onesiphorus who brought his track record of leadership skills and personal influence to our attention. It was the Apostle Paul who pointedly and publicly commended him. Without Paul's forthright expression of gratitude to Onesiphorus, we may have never heard of him or learned of his servant leadership lifestyle.

In the later stages of Paul's life, he reflected on those with whom he had significant relationships during his travels and ministry. Onesiphorus was prominently mentioned. Paul states that Onesiphorus ministered to him faithfully, consistently and regularly without public recognition, announcement or applause. Paul proceeded to publicly commend him for his faithful service to him and others. By so doing, he sets forth Onesiphorus as an example of "spreading happiness" through hospitality and encouragement.

It appears that Onesiphorus was often there to help Paul at critical times in his life. He was there especially whenever Paul needed encouragement, support and his health re-established. These usually were the times when Paul was in prison, had just been released from prison or was facing some kind of difficult circumstance. At the time, he was in need of being refreshed and to have a sense of confidence and happiness renewed within him. It was because of Onesiphorus and others that Paul was renewed so he could carry on his ministry for the gospel of Jesus Christ.

In fairly strong language and with a sense of deep appreciation and gratitude, Paul states to his friend, Timothy, that Onesiphorus was a man who possessed courage, love, boldness, and faithfulness. Paul then went on to tell Timothy that Onesiphorus "often refreshed me." No doubt Paul wanted Timothy to benefit from Onesiphorus and his household as he had so many times over the years.

Onesiphorus must have been a happy person and knew how to bring about happiness in others, in order to have that kind of positive effect on Paul and others. Thus, Paul undoubtedly felt increased happiness from the support and friendship of Onesiphorus.

In Paul's concluding and celebrating remark, we know that Paul's happiness was encouraged and facilitated by Onesiphorus. It was Onesiphorus who gave while Paul received. When Paul was in need, Onesiphorus gave to Paul from his personal resources. Paul not only enjoyed his stay but was in a stronger position to carry the gospel to many countries and people-groups because of it. Many others also became the recipients of Onesiphorus' servant leadership, unselfish hospitality, and happiness spreading. As Onesiphorus practiced and spread happiness through servant leadership and friendship, he himself reaped his share of happiness and meaningfulness. *Dare to be a faithful, happiness spreading servant like Onesiphorus to others at times of needed respite!*

FURTHER READING ON HAPPINESS SPREADING

II Timothy 1:16-18; 4:19
Nehemiah 8:10, 17-18
Psalms 97:11; 100:3
Ecclesiastes 1:16-18; 6:8
I Peter 1:8-9
Jude 24-25
Hebrews 1:9

DISCUSSION QUESTIONS

Happiness Spreading Discussion Questions

1. What do you think is the basis and essence of your personal and interpersonal happiness?

2. Reflect on a time in your life that was a happy time. Who contributed to your happiness? How did your happiness benefit others?

3. When you have a need for happiness, how do you go about generating it? Do you bring happiness to others? If so, how? Do others bring happiness to you? If so, how?

4. Which of the Happiness Arrowheads do you find personally helpful, challenging or impacting you in some way? Tell why?

Onesiphorus Discussion Questions

1. Who is a modern day example of Onesiphorus? How do you see it being lived out? How does/did this person impact your life?

2. How can we train our children to be like Onesiphorus in their adult world? Any examples?

3. Do you have a little bit of Onesiphorus within you, but you have been hesitant to act on it? Why? What is needed to help you step forward and become an Onesiphorus in your own right?

4. Did you ever have an Onesiphorus in your life? How did you benefit from this person? How did you develop such a relationship? What is the status of that relationship now?

5. In what way have you been an Onesiphorus in the life of someone else? Why did that person need or deserve such a relationship? Was it appreciated?

HAPPINESS SPREADING DAILY EXERCISES

1. Express your gratitude to someone who has touched and enriched your life in the past few years.

2. List your 5-10 closest friends; note why they are considered a friend and what they contribute to you and what you contribute to them through your friendship.

3. Become associated with a ministry or service organization and engage as Onesiphorus would have with those in a leadership position.

4. Find out where God is doing something amazing and become part of the action.

5. Write a "gratitude journal" each day by writing down one to three things for which you are thankful and that made you happy that day.

6. Engage in a "random act of kindness" each day this week by doing some kind thing for a family, friend and/or stranger.

7. Plan a way to teach your children or someone else how to live, cope, and relate to others with a "happy heart."

HAPPINESS SPREADING ARROWHEADS

- The only way to keep happiness is to give it.
- Gratitude generally gets us a second helping.
- The glow of the sunset removes the fear of night.
- True gratitude is always voluntary.
- The debts which gold can't pay would stand for aye, if we should never have Thanksgiving Day.
- We may learn three things from the honeybee: go straight, keep busy and gather but the sweets along the way.
- The closest we can come to getting everything we want is to want everything we get.
- An empty vessel draws attention to itself; a full one to its content.
- When selfishness comes in the front door, happiness goes out at the rear.
- Happiness will flee from you if you pursue it, but will pursue you if you flee from it.
- True happiness does not just happen.
- The same sunshine which inspires exclamations of joy becomes unbearable after two weeks without a cloud.
- A baby cries by nature but must be taught to smile.
- Gifts which we do not need often inspire the greatest gratitude.
- Gratitude adds a flavor to the poor man's crust which the delicacies of the king's table do not possess.

My Happiness Spreading Arrowhead _____

MY WEEKLY JOURNAL OF HAPPINESS SPREADING

The *happiness spreading* lessons I learned this week were....

APPENDIX

APPENDIX A

ASSESSING MY EMOTIONAL INTELLIGENCE

On a 10 point scale please estimate your current level of skill on each of the 15 components of emotional intelligence. Be honest with yourself in making your estimate. To help you, think of being above or below the 50% mark (5/10). Then estimate if you are at the high end or low end of the scale for each trait. Assume that a 10 is the best possible score.

Rate yourself a second time after you have read the book or portions of each chapter. Then rate yourself again after a few months of living while trying to enhance your skills of emotional intelligence.

THE TRAITS OF EMOTIONAL INTELLIGENCE

NOTES

1. Self-Respect
1___2___3___4___5___6___7___8___9___10___
   (I like myself as I am and am becoming)

2. Self-Awareness
1___2___3___4___5___6___7___8___9___10___
    (I am aware of my emotions, needs)

3. Assertive Communication
1___2___3___4___5___6___7___8___9___10___
    (I speak up for myself and my needs)

4. Independence
1___2___3___4___5___6___7___8___9___10___
    (I can act apart from social pressure)

5. Self-Actualization
1___2___3___4___5___6___7___8___9___10___
    (I strive to live beyond the present)

6. Empathic Peacemaking
1___2___3___4___5___6___7___8___9___10___
    (I act with feeling and care for others)

7. Interpersonal Sensitivity
1___2___3___4___5___6___7___8___9___10___
    (I am aware of the needs of others)

8. Interpersonal Bonding
1___2___3___4___5___6___7___8___9___10___
    (I form strong, mutual friendships)

9. Reality Awareness
1___2___3___4___5___6___7___8___9___10___
    (I know my culture and world events)

10. Flexible Decision Making
1___2___3___4___5___6___7___8___9___10___
    (I can adjust to life's changing demands)

11. Problem Solving
1___2___3___4___5___6___7___8___9___10___
    (I confront problems and solve them)

12. Stress Tolerance
1___2___3___4___5___6___7___8___9___10___
    (I can deal with pressure and conflict)

13. Impulse Control
1___2___3___4___5___6___7___8___9___10___
    (I act after thinking and planning)

14. Optimistic Thinking
1___2___3___4___5___6___7___8___9___10___
    (I view the future with positive hope)

15. Happiness Spreading
1___2___3___4___5___6___7___8___9___10___
    (I am happy and spread happiness)

Sub-Scores 1-5 =____ 6-8=____ 9-11 =____ 12-13=____ 14-15=____
Sum Total = _____

ACTION PLAN

After evaluating yourself on each of the fifteen components of emotional intelligence, plan to read and study all those chapters on which you rated yourself at a score below seven (7). If you scored yourself below a five (5) be sure to plan to spend extra time on those particular chapters and be sure to engage someone in discussing the questions and doing the homework suggestions. If you scored below three (3) look up the name of a local psychologist and engage in professional counseling on those particular subjects. This is an area of daily living that is too important to pass up or take lightly.

Yes, you can become more emotionally intelligent. However, you must be intentional and focused on the areas in which you desire to improve your emotional sensitivity, relational lifestyle and interpersonal skills.

APPENDIX B

HEALTHY INTERPERSONAL RELATIONSHIPS

Healthy interpersonal relationships are formed, shaped, matured and enjoyed. They don't develop naturally. They are intentionally developed over time and with concerted effort on the part of both or all parties. Developing relationships and friendships take time and mutual investment. Either party can squash them, terminate them, or help them flourish. Unfortunately, it is easier and quicker to terminate a relationship than it is to build a mature, satisfying and healthy long-term relationship. My long time fishing partner, Art Spierer, put it this way, *"It takes a long time to make a best friend."* How true!

Below are ten healthy patterns of interpersonal relationships based on emotional intelligence. Read each one slowly and before proceeding to the next item, evaluate how you are doing on each point. If necessary, design a plan on how you might go about improving yourself on each item on which it appears you need improvement.

THE UNWRAPPING OF INTERPERSONAL RELATIONSHIPS

1. *Give the higher value and priority to others over yourself.* Showing interest in others and becoming part of their life's journey draws a sense of togetherness and mutual appreciation. Interest in others creates a sense of respect, consideration, and compassion for others. **I'm OK___; I could improve___**

2. *Listen more than devoting time to talking.* When someone listens to us we know that they are interested in us, care about us, and want to know about us intimately. Developing strong listening skills is vital to the formation of interpersonal relationships. **I'm OK___; I could improve___**

3. *Giving is better than receiving.* The giving of time, attention, and one's personal resources for the good of others not only enriches the other person, but is the basis of receiving in return. It is always better to give than to receive. Giving for the benefit of others will always return many-fold. **I'm OK___; I could improve___**

4. *Be willing to allow the credit of admirable deeds to be bestowed upon a person.* Don't be anxious to gather credits for yourself. **I'm OK___; I could improve___**

5. *Consider the feelings and sensitivities of other people over your own.* Consider that some people are very thin skinned and are easily hurt while you may be to the contrary. Measure your words and expressions with sensitivity and thoughtfulness. In your inactions with others, keep an open mind. Be quick to listen and slow to judge. Be receptive to new ideas and learn from others while avoiding the tendency to be critical and disinterested in what others think or have to say. **I'm OK___; I could improve___**

6. *Let your virtues lead in your interactions in relationships with others.* Let your personal virtues be obvious and clear and consistently expressed and lived. **I'm OK___; I could improve___**

7. *Let the negative, critical and mean-spirited comments of others roll off your back as water rolls off the back of a duck.* To counter the critical nature of others only leads to conflict and argumentation. Take the high road. Such a comment deserves silence. **I'm OK___; I could improve___**

8. *Be positive, cheerful, and warm as you meet and interact with others.* Remember everyone is carrying a burden. **I'm OK___; I could improve___**

9. *Be an encourager where there are many opportunities to encourage others.* So be ready, be prone, to say the encouraging word at moments of defeat, despair, and hurt in the lives of others. Bridle your tongue. Remember how you say it speaks louder than what you say. Be quicker to listen than to speak. Speak with measured words, but be a ready and open conversationalist. **I'm OK___; I could improve___**

10. *Be a promise keeper.* Make few promises, but keep the ones you make. The trust factor within any relationship is based on a well established and well known record of promise keeping. **I'm OK___; I could improve___**

APPENDIX C

TIMUS LIVING SCALE

Instructions: This survey is to be completed by someone who knows the applicant fairly well. Please respond to each item using the 7 point rating scale on the right. Consider the person being rated for the time period you have known the person, but give more weight to your observations over the past 9-12 months.

Very		Very
Much	So,	Much
Untrue	So	True

1. Lives a life that is blameless and above reproach.

_____:_____:_____:_____:_____:_____:_____:

2. Lives a married life which excludes extra-marital affairs or any other non-biblical sexual conduct.

_____:_____:_____:_____:_____:_____:_____:

3. Lives a temperate and moderate lifestyle and verbal expression.

_____:_____:_____:_____:_____:_____:_____:

4. Exhibits behavioral and mood patterns which indicate favorable self-control.

_____:_____:_____:_____:_____:_____:____:

5. Lives a life which commands respect from family, close friends and associates.

_____:_____:_____:_____:_____:_____:____:

6. Known to be a person who is hospitable towards others.

_____:_____:_____:_____:_____:_____:____:

7. Possesses the ability to teach others as a group or individually.

_____:_____:_____:_____:_____:_____:____:

8. Personal habits <u>exclude</u> the consumption of alcoholic beverages.

_____:_____:_____:_____:_____:_____:____:

9. Treats other people considerately, softly and kindly.

_____:_____:_____:_____:_____:_____:____:

10. Avoids useless, quarrelsome and argumentative debate.

_____:_____:_____:_____:_____:_____:____:

11. Works diligently; has a positive work ethic and is not motivated by the love of money or greed.

_____:_____:_____:_____:_____:_____:____:

12 Manages his family life well and acts to correct the children if they are disrespectful or disobedient.

_____:_____:_____:_____:_____:_____:____:

13. Is not a recent convert to faith in Jesus Christ and has mature faith.

_____:_____:_____:_____:_____:_____:____:

14. Enjoys a good reputation with those outside the Christian faith and church.

_____:_____:_____:_____:_____:_____:____:

15. Demonstrates good judgment by avoiding things which are questionable, unseemly, and dishonorable.

_____:_____:_____:_____:_____:_____:_____:

16. Lives a life known for godliness, holiness and personal piety.

_____:_____:_____:_____:_____:_____:_____:

17. Patterns of living do not suggest selfish or dishonest gain.

_____:_____:_____:_____:_____:_____:_____:

18. Upholds entrusted confidences and respects confidential information.

_____:_____:_____:_____:_____:_____:_____:

19. Articulates sound doctrine; openly shares his Christian faith, and assists others in their pursuit of godly living and sound Biblical knowledge.

_____:_____:_____:_____:_____:_____:_____:

20. Respects the views of others; is not overbearing, dominant or excessively persuasive with others.

_____:_____:_____:_____:_____:_____:_____:

Person rated: _____

How long have you known this person?_____

Person rating: _____ Date _____

APPENDIX D

THE FORGIVENESS JOURNEY

The emotionally intelligent journey of forgiveness starts with the attitude and commitment to let go of a grudge or hurt feeling for good and in exchange for a healthier lifestyle. Forgiveness is associated with a state of quietness and calmness of mind and body. Forgiveness is a relational action and commitment that two or more people make to each other and agree to live by for the future.

Below are the steps to be taken when seeking and entering the sphere of forgiveness. This is true whether it is related to a recent hurt or a trauma that is longstanding.

The Unwrapping of Forgiveness

1. Take time to study your own feelings about a situation that happened that was hurtful and painful. Articulate what it was about the situation that was not good for you. For the few trusted people not involved in the situation, share the essence of the situation and your feelings about it.

Ask them to be confidential about your sharing this very personal and deep emotional event in your life.

2. Forgiveness is a personal action. It is for you. It is for you to relieve yourself of the deep pains of hurt, anger and resentment. Do what you have to do to feel better and be relieved of the burden of resentment.

3. When engaging in an act of forgiveness, remember that it does not mean that you are condoning what has happened or even intending on reconciling with that person or a group of people. What you are after is your own inner peace. Somebody took your peace away and you are trying to retrieve it.

4. Rework and restate your grieving experience. Give it a different perspective. Come to understand it differently. Make it less emotional and more objective.

5. Adjust your perspective on the hurt and pain that you have been feeling. Remember, your feelings, thoughts, hurt, pain, and resentment is what is distressing you, not the act that happened a few minutes earlier or years earlier. The act of forgiveness is to change the hurt feelings rather than to change the situation that happened.

6. While moving along on this journey of forgiveness, engage in various techniques and methods to manage your stress and quiet your feelings of distress and upset. Engage in deep breathing exercises, muscle relaxation exercises, calm visualizations, and repeating words of kindness, gentleness, and mercy.

7. Remember that there are "un-enforcable rules" that operate within relationships. There are people who cannot give what you feel you need or deserve or desire. They cannot improve your health or personal status in life; only you can

do that. They cannot give to you what you want and what others choose not to provide for you.

8. Back track your own personal mental tape. Instead of reversing what you feel has been an injustice and wrongful act perpetrated against you, consider ways in which you can turn that situation around and through it do something good for yourself or advance yourself as you move forward into the future. Even though something is meant for evil, make it for good, for the good of other and the good of yourself.

9. Amend your "grief story" and thereby remind yourself of the heroic deeds and efforts you did put forth in the situation, as well as what you have done to recover from the situation. Forgiveness in itself is a heroic act.

10. Keep reminding yourself that a life well lived and a life that finishes well is the best revenge in itself. Instead of focusing on the cause of your pain, and the person/ persons involved in perpetrating this painful event, look for evidence of compassion, kindness, and beauty around you, and in the lives of those with whom you have strong personal and long-term relationships. Forgiveness is about your own personal power: the power to forgive, the power to accept forgiveness, the power to look beyond the hurt and into the future, and the power to start a new journey.

Final Note

Forgive and the forgetting will take place over time, as will the rebuilding of trust.

APPENDIX E

THE TEN COMMANDMENTS OF
INTERPERSONAL RELATIONSHIPS

Interpersonal relationships are formed, shaped, matured and enjoyed. They don't develop naturally. They are intentionally developed over time and with concerted effort on the part of both or all parties. Developing relationships and friendships take time and mutual investment. Either party can squash it or terminate it. Unfortunately, it is easier and quicker to terminate a relationship than it is to build a mature, satisfying and healthy long-term relationship.

Below are the ten commandments of interpersonal relationships based on emotional intelligence.

Read each one slowly and evaluate how you are doing on each point before proceeding to the next item. If necessary, design a plan on how you might go about improving yourself on any item your think you need improvement. My fishing partner, Art Spierer, would often remind me, "*It takes a long time to make and old friend.*" Take your time, but do what is necessary to improve your relationship skills.

THE UNWRAPPING OF INTERPERSONAL RELATIONSHIPS

1. *Give the higher value and priority to others over oneself.* Showing interest in others and becoming part of their life's journey draws a sense of togetherness and mutual appreciation. Interest in others creates a sense of respect, consideration, and compassion for others.

2. *Listen more than devoting time to talking.* When someone listens to us we know that they are interested in us, care about us, and want to know about us intimately. Developing strong listening skills is vital to the formation of interpersonal relationships.

3. *Giving is better than receiving.* The giving of time, attention, and one's personal resources for the good of others not only enriches the other person, but is the basis of receiving in return. It is always better to give than to get. Giving for the benefit of others will always return tenfold.

4. *Be willing to allow the credit of admirable deeds to be bestowed upon another person.* Don't be anxious to gather credits for oneself.

5. *Consider the feelings and sensitivities of other people over your one.* Consider that some people are very thin skinned and are easily hurt while you may be to the contrary. Measure your words and expressions with sensitivity and thoughtfulness. In your inactions with others, keep an open mind. Be quick to listen and slow to judge. Be receptive to new ideas and learn from others while avoiding the tendency to be critical and disinterested in what others think or have to say.

6. *Let your virtues lead in your interactions in relationships with others.* Let your personal virtues be obvious and clear and consistently expressed and lived.

7. *Let the negative, critical and mean-spirited comments of others roll off your back* as. *water rolls off the back of a duck.* To counter the critical nature of others only leads to conflict and argumentation. Take the high road. Such a comment deserves silence.

8. *Be positive, cheerful, and warm as you meet and interact with others.* Remember everyone is carrying a burden.

9. *Be an encourager where there are many opportunities to encourage others.* So be ready, be prone, to say the encouraging word at moments of defeat, despair, and hurt in the lives of others. Bridle your tongue. Remember how you say it speaks louder than what you say. Be quicker to listen than to speak. Speak with measured words, but as a conversationalist.

10. *Be a promise keeper.* Make few promises, but keep them. The trust in any relationship is based on promise keeping.

APPENDIX F

HOW TO READ THIS BOOK

Most books are written to be read in sequence, beginning to end. Not this one. Read the preface. First, emotional intelligence must be understood. The components of emotional intelligence also must be reviewed and understood. However, the book can be read as the reader's needs and interests dictate. Each chapter presents a component of emotional intelligence and each chapter stands on its own. Each chapter can be helpful to the person's development even if read separately.

Each chapter identifies one of the emotional intelligence components. Each component is then amplified. Each component is discussed as to how it can be achieved or lived out through the example of a biblical character. It is anticipated that the real life examples will help the reader see life more clearly and how to live more effectively and harmoniously.

Lastly, each component is captured in a list of quotations from the book, *ARROW-HEADS: Some Straight Lines for Strong Living,* authored by Rev. Fred Beck. Arrowheads are quotes, adages or phrases that teach a basic moralism or principle essential to living an emotionally intelligent life. They are mini-lessons on life.

As you read, use the book as a reference tool. Let your interests and needs determine your reading, what you learn, and what you apply from it. For example, should you, or your child, for example, need to improve in one of the areas of interpersonal skills, read all three sections under the general topic of Interpersonal Relationships? Likewise, if mood management is an area needing improvement, read the two topics under Mood Management.

Remember, all fifteen chapters teach and unfold the meaning of emotional intelligence. We need to be as behaviorally competent as possible in each of the fifteen areas of emotional intelligence so we can live effectively and competently in our social world.

IF YOU ARE LEADING A BIBLE STUDY

If you lead a Bible study or teach a Sunday School class, this book will take you and the group on a step by step journey into the Bible and the lives of 15 primary Biblical leaders. As you follow the lead of these Biblical leaders, you will come to learn and apply the basic tenets of emotional intelligence. Your life and that of the group will be enriched and your mutual interpersonal effectiveness will develop and strengthen.

IF YOU ARE IN COUNSELING

If you are consulting a professional therapist, ask the therapist to look over the book and pinpoint for you those areas in which you need improvement. Discuss how counseling can be helpful to you as you focus on certain areas of personal improvement. Let the book be your counseling text and primary reference during therapy. Select a few chapters to go over together during a few sessions.

IF YOU ARE A PARENT, TEACHER OR CHILD CARE WORKER

Consider the book a primary reference for helping plan lessons and learn how to interact with the children for whom you are responsible as a parent, teacher or youth leader. It is best for children to learn the skills of emotional intelligence early in life. If so, they will be better prepared for what is ahead of them. Their potential for achievement will be increased. Their spiritual meaning in life will be enhanced and more personal. Their social skills will be improved. Their resistance to negative temptation will be stronger. And their resistance to the adverse affects of stress will be greater.

IF YOU ARE A PASTOR OR PUBLIC SPEAKER

The book will be found to be valuable for pastors and others who do public speaking. As a pastor focus on or utilize the concepts of emotional intelligence in your sermons. The book models how each one of the traits of emotional intelligence can be amplified. It then illustrates each trait in the life of a biblical character. Help give your congregation a feel for the emotional experiences of biblical characters.

IF YOU ARE A STUDENT

Use this book for your own personal growth. Read it for extra reading. Through your reading learn how to be socially competent and socially accepted. Use as a tool to learn biblical history through the life stories of the biblical characters presented in each chapter.

IF YOU ARE A SEEKER AFTER GODLY LIVING

LIVING LIFE @ ITS BEST is a book worth reading for the following reasons:

1. It will help you gain greater insight into the lives of Biblical characters.

2. It will help you integrate Biblical truths into everyday living.

3. It will help you improve your social skills with those with whom you socially interact each day.

4. It will help you improve your competitive advantage in your business and social world.

5. It will help you improve your effectiveness in daily living.

6. It will help you adjust and adapt to the world around you.

7. It will help you be effective as a leader/or as agent of change in your sphere of influence.

Enjoy the journey . . . . and share *LIVING LIFE @ ITS BEST* with others. Engage others in a small group for study and discussion, using the book as a text.

APPENDIX G

PREVIOUS BOOKS BY DR. HEDBERG

Hedberg, A., *Doctor Teach Me to Parent,* AuthorHouse, 2013

Hedberg, A., *Lessons From My Father,* Crossbooks, 2012

Hedberg, A., *Achieving and Maintaining a Healthy Lifestyle in a World of Stress*, AuthorHouse, 2012

Hedberg, A., *Forms for the Therapist*, Elsevier Press, 2010

Walker, G., Clement, Hedberg, A., *Strategies in Behavior Therapy*, Prentice-Hall, 1981

Hedberg, A., *Depression: Positive Strategies for Change*, Self-Control Press, 1981

Hedberg, A. and Walker, E., *Clinical Psychology: Is There a Place for Me?* American Psychological Association, Division 12, 1973